For
MICHAEL SMITH, poet

Stoned to death on Stony Hill
Kingston, Jamaica

17 August 1983

And what does that mean: Congo. What does it mean when
   you say Congo?
Congo is the nation
Which nation, the Congo nation?
The Congo nation
And people here know what nation they belong to?
Yes. Everybody know what is a nation . . .
What is your nation?
Kromantee and Tembe
Are you a Congo?
Kromantee . . .

                              Alan Lomax in Carriacou in the 1950s

What I am going to talk about this morning is language from the Caribbean, the process of using English in a different way from the 'norm'. English in a new sense as I prefer to call it. English in an ancient sense. English in a very traditional sense. And sometimes not English at all, but *language*.

I start my thoughts, taking up from the discussion that developed after Dennis Brutus's* very excellent presentation. Without logic, and through instinct, the people who spoke with Dennis from the floor yesterday brought up the question of language. Actually, Dennis's presentation had nothing to do with language. He was speaking about the structural condition of South Africa. But instinctively people recognized that the structural condition described by Dennis had very much to do with language. He didn't concentrate on the language aspect of it because there wasn't enough time and because it was not his main concern. But it was interesting that your instincts, not your logic, moved you toward the question of the relationship between language and culture, language and structure. In his case, it was English as spoken by Africans, and the native languages as spoken by Africans.

We in the Caribbean have a similar kind of plurality : we have English, which is the imposed language on much of the archipelago. It is an imperial language, as are French, Dutch and Spanish. We also have what we call creole English, which is a mixture of English and an adaptation that English took in the new environment of the Caribbean when it became mixed with the other imported languages. We have also what is called *nation language,* which is the kind of English spoken by the people who were brought to the Caribbean, not the official English now, but the language of slaves and labourers, the ser-

---

* Dennis Brutus, the South African poet-and-activist-in-exile. His presentation preceded mine at this Conference and was part of a Third World segment : Azanian Caribbean and Navajo.

vants who were brought in by the conquistadors. Finally, we have the remnants of ancestral languages still persisting in the Caribbean. There is Amerindian, which is active in certain parts of Central America but not in the Caribbean because the Amerindians are here a destroyed people, and their languages were practically destroyed. We have Hindi, spoken by some of the more traditional East Indians who live in the Caribbean, and there are also varieties of Chinese.[1] And, miraculously, there are survivals of African languages still persisting in the Caribbean. So we have that spectrum—that prism—of languages similar to the kind of structure that Dennis described for South Africa. Now, I have to give you some kind of background to the development of these languages, the historical development of this plurality, because I can't take it for granted that you know and understand the history of the Caribbean.

The Caribbean is a set of islands stretching out from Florida in a mighty curve. You must know of the Caribbean at least from television, at least now with hurricane David* coming right into it. The islands stretch out on an arc of some two thousand miles from Florida through the Atlantic to the South American coast, and they were originally inhabited by Amerindian people: Taino, Siboney, Carib, Arawak. In 1492 Columbus 'discovered' (as it is said) the Caribbean, and with that discovery came the intrusion of European culture and peoples and a fragmentation of the original Amerindian culture. We had Europe 'nationalizing' itself into Spanish, French, English and Dutch so that

---

* This talk was presented at Harvard University, Cambridge, Massachusetts, late in August 1979. Hurricanes ravish the Caribbean and the southern coasts of the United States every summer. David (1979) was followed by Allen (1980) one of the most powerful on record.

1. No one, as far as I know, has yet made a study of the influence of Asiatic languages on the contemporary Caribbean, and even the African impact is still in its study's infancy. For aspects of (anglophone) Caribbean cultural development relevant to this study, see my *Contradictory omens: cultural diversity and integration in the Caribbean* (Savacou Publications, Mona, 1974). For individual territories, see Baxter (1970), Brathwaite (1979), Nettleford (1978), Seymour (1977). See also Norman E. Whitten & John F. Szwed (eds.), *Afro-American anthropology* (New York & London 1970).

people had to start speaking (and *thinking*) four metropolitan languages rather than possibly a single native language. Then with the destruction of the Amerindians, which took place within 30 years of Columbus' discovery (one million dead a year) it was necessary for the Europeans to import new labour bodies into the area. And the most convenient form of labour was the labour on the edge of the *slave* trade winds, the labour on the edge of the hurrican, the labour on the ledge of Africa. And so Ashanti, Congo, Yoruba, all that mighty coast of western Africa was imported into the Caribbean. And we had the arrival in our area of a new language structure. It consisted of many languages but basically they had a common semantic and stylistic form.[2] What these languages had to do, however, was to submerge themselves, because officially the conquering peoples—the Spaniards, the English, the French, and the Dutch—insisted that the language of public discourse and conversation, of obedience, command and conception should be English, French, Spanish or Dutch. They did not wish to hear people speaking Ashanti or any of the Congolese languages. So there was a submergence of this imported language. Its status became one of inferiority. Similarly, its speakers were slaves. They were conceived of as inferiors—non-human, in fact. But this very submergence served an interesting interculturative purpose, because although people continued to speak English as it was spoken in Elizabethan times and on through the Romantic and Victorian ages, that English was, nonetheless, still being influenced by the underground language, the submerged language that the slaves had brought. And that underground language was itself constantly transforming itself into new forms. It was moving from a purely African form to a form which was African but which was adapted to the new environment and adapted to the cultural imperative of the European languages. And it was influencing the way in which the English, French, Dutch, and Spaniards spoke their own

---

2. See Alan Lomax, 'Africanisms in New World Negro music: a canto-metric analysis', *Research and Resources of Haiti* (New York 1969), *The Haitian potential* (New York 1975); Mervyn Alleyne 'The linguistic continuity of Africa in the Caribbean', *Black Academy Review* 1 (4), Winter 1970, pp. 3-16 and *Comparative Afro-American: an historical-comparative study of English-based Afro-American dialects of the New World* (Ann Arbor 1980).

languages. So there was a very complex process taking place, which is now beginning to surface in our literature.

Now, as in South Africa (and any area of cultural imperialism for that matter), the educational system of the Caribbean did not recognize the presence of these various languages. What our educational system did was to recognize and maintain the language of the conquistador—the language of the planter, the language of the official, the language of the anglican preacher. It insisted that not only would English be spoken in the anglophone Caribbean, but that the educational system would carry the contours of an English heritage. Hence, as Dennis said, Shakespeare, George Eliot, Jane Austen—British literature and literary forms, the models which had very little to do, really, with the environment and the reality of non-Europe — were dominant in the Caribbean educational system. It was a very surprising situation. People were forced to learn things which had no relevance to themselves. Paradoxically, in the Caribbean (as in many other 'cultural disaster' areas), the people educated in this system came to know more, even today, about English kings and queens than they do about our own national heroes, our own slave rebels, the people who helped to build and to destroy our society. We are more excited by their literary models, by the concept of, say, Sherwood Forest and Robin Hood than we are by Nanny of the Maroons,[3] a name some of us didn't even know until a few years ago. And in terms of what we write, our perceptual models, we are more conscious (in terms of sensibility) of the falling of snow, for instance—the models are all there for the falling of the snow—than of the force of the hurricanes which take place every year. In other words, we haven't got the syllables, the syllabic intelligence, to describe the hurricane,[4] which is our own experience, whereas we can describe the

---

3. The Maroons were Africans/escaped slaves who, throughout Plantation America, set up autonomous societies, as a result of successful runaway and/or rebellion in 'marginal', certainly inaccessible, areas outside European influence. See Richard Price (ed.), *Maroon societies* (New York 1973). Nanny of the Maroons, an ex-Ashanti (?) Queen Mother, is regarded as one of the greatest of the Jamaica freedom fighters. See Brathwaite, *Wars of respect* (Kingston 1977).

4. But see Tony Hinkson's poem, below.

8

imported alien experience of the snowfall. It is that kind of situation that we are in.

> The day the first snow fell I floated to my birth
> of feathers falling by my window; touched earth
> and melted, touched again and left a little touch of light
> and everywhere we touched till earth was white.'

This is why there were (are?) Caribbean children who, instead of writing in their 'creole' essays 'the snow was falling on the playing fields of Shropshire' (which is what our children literally were writing until a few years ago, below drawings they made of white snowfields and the corn-haired people who inhabited such a landscape), wrote: *'the snow was falling on the canefields'* :' trying to have both cultures at the same time.

What is even more important, as we develop this business of emergent language in the Caribbean, is the actual rhythm and the syllables, the very software, in a way, of the language. What English has given us as a model for poetry, and to a lesser extent prose (but poetry is the basic tool here), is the pentameter : 'The cúrfew tólls the knéll of párting dáy'. There have, of course, been attempts to break it. And there were other dominant forms like, for example, *Beowulf* (c.750), *The Seafarer* and what Langland (?1332-?1400) had produced :

> For trewthe telleth that loue. is triacle of hevene;
> May no synne be on him sene. that useth that spise,
> And alle his werkes he wrougte. with loue as him liste

or, from *Piers the Plowman* (which does not make it into *Palgrave's Golden Treasury* which we all had to 'do' at school) the haunting prologue :

> In a somer seson. whan soft was the sonne
> I shope me into shroudes. as I a shepe were

---

5. Edward Kamau Brathwaite, 'The day the first snow fell', *Delta* (Cambridge, England [1951]), *Other exiles* (London 1975), p.7.
6. I am indebted to Anne Walmsley, editor of the anthology *The sun's eye* (London 1968) for this example. For experiences of teachers trying to cope with West Indian English in Britain, see Chris Searle, *The forsaken lover: white words and black people* (London 1972) and *Okike* (15 August 1979).

which has recently inspired Derek Walcott with his first major nation language effort :

> In idle August, while the sea soft,
> and leaves of brown islands stick to the rim
> of this Caribbean, I blow out the light
> by the dreamless face of Maria Concepcion
> to ship as a seaman on the schooner *Flight*.[7]

But by the time we reach Chaucer (1345-1400) the pentameter prevails. Over in the New World, the Americans—Walt Whitman—tried to bridge or to break the pentameter through a cosmic movement, a large movement of sound. cummings tried to fragment it. And Marianne Moore attacked it with syllabics. But basically the pentameter remained, and it carries with it a certain kind of experience, which is not the experience of a hurricane. The hurricane does not roar in pentameters. And that's the problem : how do you get a rhythm which approximates the *natural* experience, the *environmental* experience?

> God talk to de fowl cocks
> early dat mornin
> he tell dem not to crow
> so silence come on
> possess ever wing
> and fear ever feather
>
> *What is dis . . .*
>
> an de quarrelsome shack-shack
> tongue tight
> an de howlin mile tree
> quiet quiet

---

7. Derek Walcott, 'The schooner *Flight*', *The star-apple kingdom* (New York 1979; London 1980), p.3. Langland's prelude to *Piers* is often 'softened' into 'In somer season, whan soft was the sonne/I shope me in shroudes as I shepe were', which places it closer to Walcott—and to the pentameter.

and de dancin palm tree
hand fold
witholdin duh spirit

Man better take warnin

an dawn
like it smell a rat
cautious bout what comin
like it smell a rat
backin back
like a cat
over house
over tree
backin back under sea

an star an moon
heads covered
turn back to duh beds
an so
jus' so
before grasshopper could blink 'e eye
de whole sky shut up
just so
in terror an
den de news break

> *Hurry man*
> *Hurry chile*
> *Hurry lan'*
> *While you can*

Hurricane!

Anthony Hinkson (Barbados) catches, like no-one else I know, the foreboding of the hurricane, but when the hurricane itself comes, when 'leaves collapse' and 'ever man turn owl/ever jack/eye wide/mout twist in surprise', not even Hinkson can catch all the right syllables :

11

Sirens
Churchbells
Swells o' panic
bustle
bustle
quick quick to de church
mek fuh de shelter
Oh lawd
oh lawd
as de first branch fall'

In 1961, there appeared in *Leewards: writings, past and present about the Leeward Islands,* collected and edited by John Brown, Resident Tutor, Leeward Islands, UCWI, 'Two poems for Anguilla after Hurricane Donna', September 1960 (pp.57-59). One of them, by Anne Nunn (creole? or a visitor? the Hopkins model suggests a visitor), gets to the *effect* of the hurricane :

> That hurricane, he came drummed on
> My door, bowled the whole shack
> Head over heels, cracked
> Concrete like biscuit, broke
> Bed and bone . . .⁹

But still no 'proper' *hurricane;* no volcano except Shake Keane's *Volcano Suite* (1979) no earthquake; drought only in Walcott and Brathwaite's *Islands* (1969) and *Black + Blues* (1976), fire in Walcott's 'A city's death by fire' (1948) and (a fuller treatment of the Castries event) in *Another life* (1973 Ch. 13) and (as cannesbrulées) again in Brathwaite's *Islands* . . . But we have been trying to break out of the entire pentametric model in the Caribbean and to move into a system which more closely and intimately approaches our own experience. So that is what we are talking about now.

---

8. Anthony Hinkson, 'Janet', *Slavation,* unpub. coll. [Bridgetown 1976].
9. Anne Nunn, 'Donna', in John Brown (ed.), *Leewards: writings past and present* . . . ([Basseterre, St. Kitts] 1961), p.57.

2

It is *nation language* in the Caribbean that, in fact, largely ignores the pentameter. Nation language is the language which is influenced very strongly by the African model, the African aspect of our New World/Caribbean heritage. English it may be in terms of some of its lexical features. But in its contours, its rhythm and timbre, its sound explosions, it is not English, even though the words, as you hear them, might be English to a greater or lesser degree. And this brings us back to the question that some of you raised yesterday: can English be a revolutionary language? And the lovely answer that came back was: *it is not English that is the agent. It is not language, but people, who make revolutions.*

I think, however, that language does really have a role to play here, certainly in the Caribbean. But it is an English which is not the standard, imported, educated English, but that of the submerged, surrealist experience and sensibility, which has always been there and which is now increasingly coming to the surface and influencing the perception of contemporary Caribbean people. It is what I call, as I say, *nation language*. I use the term in contrast to *dialect*. The word 'dialect' has been bandied about for a long time, and it carries very pejorative overtones. Dialect is thought of as 'bad English'. Dialect is 'inferior English'. Dialect is the language used when you want to make fun of someone. Caricature speaks in dialect. Dialect has a long history coming from the plantation where people's dignity is distorted through their language and the descriptions which the dialect gave to them. Nation language, on the other hand, is the *submerged* area of that dialect which is much more closely allied to the African aspect of experience in the Caribbean. It may be in English: but often it is in an English which is like a howl, or a shout or a machine-gun or the wind or a wave. It is also like the blues. And sometimes it is English and African at the same time. I am going to give you some examples. But I should tell you that the reason I have to talk so much is that there has been very little written on this subject. I bring to you the notion of nation language but I can refer you to very little literature, to very few resources. I cannot refer you to what you call an 'Establishment'.

I cannot really refer you to Authorities because there aren't any.[10] One of our urgent tasks now is to try to create our own Authorities. But I will give you a few ideas of what people have tried to do.

The forerunner of all this was of course Dante Alighieri who at the beginning of the fourteenth century argued, in *De vulgari eloquentia* (1304), for the recognition of the (his own) Tuscan vernacular as the nation language to replace Latin as the most natural, complete and accessible means of verbal expression. And the movement was in fact successful throughout Europe with the establishment of national languages and literatures. But these very successful national languages then proceeded to ignore local European colonials such as Basque and Gaelic, for instance, and suppressed overseas colonials wherever they were heard. And it was not until Burns in the 18th century and Rothenberg, Trask, Vansina, Tedlock, Waley, Walton, Whallon, Jahn, Jones, Whiteley, Beckwith, Herskovits, and Ruth Finnegan, among many others in this century, that we have returned, at least, to the *notion* of oral literature. Although I don't need to remind you that oral literature is our oldest form of literature and that it continues richly throughout the world today.[11] In the Caribbean, our novelists have always been conscious of these native resources, but the critics and academics have, as is kinda often the case, lagged far behind. Indeed, until 1970, there was a positive intellectual, almost social, hostility to the concept of 'dialect' as language. But there were some significant studies in linguistics : Beryl Loftman Bailey's *Jamaican creole syntax: a transformational approach* (Cambridge 1966), F. G. Cassidy, *Jamaica talk* (Kingston 1961), Cassidy and R. B. LePage *Dictionary of Jamaican English* (Cambridge 1967); and, still to come, Richard Allsopp's mind-blowing, *Dictionary of Caribbean English;* three glossaries from Frank Collymore in Barbados, and A. J. Seymour and John R. Rickford of Guyana; plus studies on the African

---

10. But see the paragraphs (and notes) that follow.
11. See for example Finnegan (1970, 1977, 1977), Andrzejewski (1964), Vansina (1961), Babalola (1966), McLuhan (1962), Nketia (1955), Opie (1967), Ogot (1967), Ogotemmeli (1948), Rothenberg (1968), Beier (1970), Tedlock (1972), Egudu & Nwoga (1973), Miss Queenie (1971) and the wonderfully rich literature on Black Culture in the Americas. See Bibliography for details of these and other references.

presence in Caribbean language by Mervyn Alleyne, Beverley Hall, and Maureen Warner Lewis.[12] In addition, there has been work by Douglas Taylor and Cicely John, among others, on aspects of some of the Amerindian languages; and Dennis Craig, Laurence Carrington, Velma Pollard and several others, at the University of the West Indies' School of Education, on the structure of nation language and its psychosomosis in and for the classroom.

Few of the writers mentioned, however, have gone into nation language as it affects literature.[13] They have set out its grammar, syntax, transformation, structure and all of those things. But

12. Frank Collymore, *Notes for a glossary of words and phrases of Barbadian dialect* (Bridgetown 1955, with several rev. and expanded editions); A. J. Seymour, *Dictionary of Guyanese folklore* (Georgetown 1975); John R. Rickford (ed.) *A festival of Guyanese words* (U of Guyana 1976, 1978); Mervyn Alleyne, 'The cultural matrix of Caribbean dialects', unpub., paper, UWI, Mona, n.d., 'What is "Jamaican" in our language?' a review of Cassidy/LePage's *Dictionary* in *Sunday Gleaner*, 9 July 1967, *Comparative Afro-American* (Ann Arbor 1980); Maureen Warner Lewis (sometimes as Warner), 'African feasts in Trinidad', *ASAWI Bulletin* 4 (1971), 'Africans in 19th century Trinidad', ibid. 5(1972), 6(1973), 'Trinidad Yoruba — notes on survival' *Caribbean Quarterly* 17:2(1971), *The nkuyu: spirit messengers of the kumina* (Mona 1977), also in *Savacou 13* (1977), *Notes to Masks [a study of Edward Kamau Brathwaite's poem]* (Benin City 1977); Edward Kamau Brathwaite, 'Brother Mais [a study of Roger Mais' novel, *Brother Man*]', *Tapia* 27 Oct 1974 and as Introduction (earlier version) to *Brother Man* (London 1974), 'Jazz and the West Indian novel', *Bim* 44-46 (1967-68), 'The African presence in Caribbean literature', *Daedalus* (Spring 1974), reprinted in Sidney Mintz (ed.), *Slavery, colonialism and racism* (New York 1974) and trans. Spanish in Manuel Moreno Fraginals (ed.) *Africa en America Latina* (Paris 1977), 'Kumina: the spirit of African survival in Jamaica', *Jamaica Journal* 42(Sept 1978) and (earlier version) in *The African Dispersal* (q.v.).
13. A special exception has to be made of the work of Roger D. Abrahams (see *Bibliography*) whose work on Caribbean and New World speech drama is invaluable pioneering. But no one else has (yet) followed and there has (so far) been no connection between Abrahams' sociocultural sense of rhetoric/imagination and our linguists, socio-linguists, sociologists and literary critics. Nor has the link between Nketia, say, and Abrahams been appreciated; though recent work by Velma Pollard (see especially her 'Dread Talk' in *Bibliography*) feels like its lighting a match . . .
I should also like to invoke J. J. Williams', *Psychic phenomena of Jamaica* (New York 1934). But that is another story. Perhaps another book.

15

they haven't really been able to make any contact between the nation language and its expression in our literature. Recently, a French poet and novelist from Martinique, Edouard Glissant, had a very remarkable article in *Alcheringa*, a 'nation language' journal published at Boston University. The article was called 'Free and Forced Poetics', and in it, for the first time, I feel an effort to describe what nation language really means. For the author of the article it is the language of enslaved persons. For him, nation language is a strategy: the slave is forced to use a certain kind of language in order to disguise himself, to disguise his personality and to retain his culture. And he defines that language as a 'forced poetics' because it is a kind of prison language, if you want to call it that.[14] And then we have another nation language poet, Bruce St John, from Barbados, who has written some informal introductions to his own work which describe the nature of the experiments that he is conducting and the kind of rules that he begins to perceive in the way that he uses his language.[15] I myself have an article called 'Jazz and the West Indian novel', which appeared in a journal called *Bim* in the early 1960s,[16] and there I attempt to show that a very necessary connection to the understanding of nation language is betwen native musical structures and the native language. That music is, in fact, the surest threshold to the language which comes out of it.[17]

In terms of more formal literary criticism, the pioneers have been H. P. Jacobs (1949) on V. S. Reid, Mervyn Morris (1964)

---

14. *Alcheringa*, New Series 2:2 (1976).
15. See Bruce St John, Introduction to his 'Bumbatuk' poems in *Revista de letras* (U of Puerto Rico en Mayaguez, 1972).
16. See Brathwaite, n.12, above.
17. Extended versions of this lecture attempt to demonstrate the link between music and language structures e.g. Brathwaite and *kaiso, aladura, sookee,* sermon, bop post-bop; Shake Keane on jazz (he is a jazz trumpeter), *cadence, anansesem;* Kwesi Johnson, Oku Onuora and reggae/dub, Michael Smith and ring-game and drumbeat, Malik *kaiso* and worksong, Keens-Douglas and *conte,* Miss Lou folksay and street shout, St John and litany. Recent developments in kaiso (Shadow/*Bass man,* Short Shirt/*Tourist leggo,* Sparrow/*Music an rhythm: How you jammin so*) suggest even more complex sound shape developments . . .

on Louise Bennett and most of Gordon Rohlehr's work, beginning with 'Sparrow and the language of calypso' (1967).[17a]

And that is all we have to offer as Authority, which isn't very much, really. But, in fact, one characteristic of nation language is its orality. It is from 'the oral tradition'. And therefore you wouldn't really expect that large, encyclopedic body of learned comment on it that you would expect for a written language and literature.

3

Now I'd like to describe for you some of the characteristics of our nation language. First of all, it is from, as I've said, an oral tradition. The poetry, the culture itself, exists not in a dictionary but in the tradition of the spoken word. It is based as much on sound as it is on song. That is to say, the noise that it makes is part of the meaning, and if you ignore the noise (or what you would *think* of as noise, shall I say) then you lose part of the meaning. When it is written, you lose the sound or the noise, and therefore you lose part of the meaning. Which is, again, why I have to have a tape recorder for this presentation. I want you to get the sound of it, rather than the sight of it.

In order to break down the pentameter, we discovered an ancient form which was always there, the calypso.[18] This is a form that I think nearly everyone knows about. It does not employ the iambic pentameter. It employs dactyls. It therefore mandates the use of the tongue in a certain way, the use of sound in a certain way. It is a model that we are moving naturally towards now. Compare

---

17a. See H. P. Jacobs, 'The Dialect of Victor Reid' *West Indian Review,* May 1949, pp.12-15; Mervyn Morris, 'On Reading Louise Bennett, seriously', *Sunday Gleaner* June 7-28, 1964, *Jamaica Journal,* Dec. 1967, pp.69-74; Gordon Rohlehr, *CAM Newsletter 2* (April/May 1967), *Savacou 2* (Sept. 1970), pp.87-99.

18. The calypso (kaiso) is well treated, in historical and musicological perspective in *Caribbean Quarterly* 4(1956) and by J. D. Elder (1970) and Errol Hill (1972). But it is Gordon Rohlehr, a critic and Reader

(IP)   To be or not to be, that is the question

(Kaiso)   The stone had skidded arc'd and bloomed into islands
          Cuba San Domingo
          Jamaica Puerto Rico[18a]

But not only is there a difference in syllabic or stress pattern, there is an important difference in shape of intonation. In the Shakespeare (IP above), the voice travels in a single forward plane towards the horizon of its end. In the kaiso, after the skimming movement of the first line, we have a distinct variation. The voice dips and deepens to describe an intervallic pattern. And then there are more ritual forms like *kumina*, like *shango*, the religious forms,[19] which I won't have time to go into here, but which begin to disclose the complexity that is possible with nation language.

The other thing about nation language is that it is part of what may be called *total expression,* a notion which is not unfamiliar to you because you are coming back to that kind of thing now. Reading is an isolated, individualistic expression. The oral tradition on the other hand demands not only the griot but the audience to complete the community : the noise and sounds

---

in English at the UWI, St Augustine, Trinidad, who apart from a few comments by C.L.R. James and Derek Walcott, is almost the only major Caribbean writer to have dealt with its literary aspects and with the relationship between kaiso (and reggae) and literature. Among his articles: 'Sparrow and the language of calypso', *CAM Newsletter* 2(1967), *Savacou* 2 (Sept 1970); 'Calypso and morality', *Moko* 17 June 1969; 'The calypso as rebellion', S.A.G. 3(1970); 'Sounds and Pressure: Jamaican Blues', *Cipriani Labour College Review,* (Jan 1970); 'Calypso and politics', *Moko* 29 Oct 1971; 'Forty years of calypso', *Tapia* 3, 17 Sept, 8 Oct 1972: 'Samuel Selvon and the language of the people' in Edward Baugh (ed.) *Critics on Caribbean literature* (London 1978), from 'The folk in Caribbean literature', *Tapia* 17 Dec 1972.

18a. Brathwaite, 'Caribbean theme: a calypso', CQ4:3&4(1956)p.246; *Rights of passage* (1967: as 'Calypso'), p.48; sung by the author on Argo DA101(1969), PLP1110(1972).

19. See G. E. Simpson, *Religious cults of the Caribbean* (Rio Piedras 1970); Honor Ford-Smith, 'The performance aspect of kumina ritual', Seminar Paper, Dept of English, UWI, Mona (1976) and Brathwaite and Warner Lewis as at n.12, above.

18

that the maker makes are responded to by the audience and are returned to him. Hence we have the creation of a continuum where meaning truly resides. And this *total expression* comes about because people be in the open air, because people live in conditions of poverty ('unhouselled') because they come from a historical experience where they had to rely on their very *breath* rather than on paraphernalia like books and museums and machines. They had to depend on *immanence,* the power within themselves, rather than the technology outside themselves.

4

Let me begin by playing you, first of all, some West Indian poets who are writing in standard English, or if you like, in *West Indian standard English.* The first poet is Claude McKay, who some people think of as American. He appears in American anthologies, especially of Black Writing. (Until recently, American anthologies hardly ever contained black writers, except perhaps Phillis Wheatley.) But McKay (1889-1940) was born in Jamaica and was a policeman in the constabulary there for some years before emigrating to the States where he quickly became a leading figure in what has come to be known as the Harlem Renaissance. But although he is very much identified with the black movement, McKay, except perhaps for the most productive years of his life, was rather ambivalent about his negritude.[20] In this recording, made towards the end of his life in the forties, when he had moved from Communism to Catholicism, he is saying, in the lead-in to his most famous and militant poem 'If we must die', that he is a *poet,* not a *black* poet, not, as he said in those days, a 'coloured' poet. And he goes on to recount the story of how a copy of 'If we must die' was found on the body of a dead (white) soldier during the First World War. The newspapers recorded the occasion and everyone started quoting the poem. But no one, McKay says, said—'perhaps they did not even know,' he says—that he was black. Which was okay by

---

20. See Wayne F. Cooper, *The passion of Claude McKay* (New York 1973).

him, he says, because it helped ensure his 'universality'. (Winston Churchill also quoted this poem—without attribution to the author who, when he had gone to Bernard Shaw for encouragement in earlier days, had been advised by that Grand Old Man (after taking a shrewd look at him) that he'd better try it as a boxer!)

Well, that's the first stage and story of our literature. We *want* to be universal, to be universally accepted. But it's the terrible terms meted out for universality that interest me. In order to be 'universal' McKay forsook his nation language, forsook his early mode of poetry,[21] and went to the sonnet. And his sonnet,

---

21. McKay's first two books of poetry (1912), written in Jamaica, are unique in that they are the first all-dialect collections from an anglophone Caribbean poet. They are however *dialect* as distinct from *nation* because McKay allowed himself to be imprisoned in the pentameter; he didn't let his language find its own parameters; though this raises the tricky question of *critical relativity:* could McKay, in the Jamaica of 1912, have done it any differently, with a svengali like Walter Jekyll, for instance, plus his *Dan-is-the-man-in-the-van* school-teacher brother? We can certainly note the results of his literary colonialism in the primordial (?) anglicanism of *Constab ballads* (London 1912) and *Songs of Jamaica* (Kingston 1912):

> I've a longin' in me dept's of heart dat I can conquer not,
> 'Tis a wish dat I've been havin' from since I could form a t'o't . . .

> Just to view de homeland England, in de streets of London walk,
> An' to see de famous sights dem 'bouten which dere's so much
> > talk . . .

('Old England', *Songs,* p.63).

By the time we reach Louise Bennett in the forties there is much less of a problem. Though the restrictive forms are still there, there is a world of difference in the activity of the language, and one suspects that *in performance* this very 'restriction' (the formal meter) is an aid to memory. Other less adventurous spirits in the fifties attempted dialect in their first editions but revised them 'upward' in subsequent versions. We are fortunate to have for purposes of comparison, in N. R. Millington's *Lingering thoughts* ([Bridgetown] 1954), two versions of 'On return from a foreign land' (the dialect entirely absent from subsequent editions).

> Oh, what a rare delight
> To see you once again!
> Your kindly, strong, familiar face
> Comes easily to my remembrance.

'St Isaac's Church, Petrograd', is a poem which could have been written by a European, perhaps most intimately by a Russian in Petrograd. It certainly could have been written by any poet of the post-Victorian era. The only thing that retains its uniqueness here (in terms of my notion of nation language) is the *tone* of the poet's voice. But the form and the content are very closely connected to European models. This does not mean that it is a bad poem or that I am putting it down. I am merely saying that aesthetically there are no unique elements in this poem apart from the *voice* of the poet reciting his own poem. And I will have a musical model which will appear after you have listened to the poem, and you can tell me whether you think I am fair or not. (On tape: McKay reading his sonnet followed by the 'Agnus Dei' from Fauré's *Requiem*.)

Our last meeting was on Roebuck Street
Which used to be so rutty.
The mule-drawn car is gone;
Gone, too, the railway;
Running on the tarmac
Are the fussy buses.
Small estates are combining into large . . .

(p.40).

"Who you and whay you come from?
Yuh voice soun' Bajan
An' yuh face familiuh.
Las' time I see yuh was 'pon Roebuck Street,
Dat use' to be suh full o' holes.
But now uh hear dat all de roads been tar
De tramcars gone, de train gone too
An' buses runnin' everywhay
At any owuh o' de day.
De little estates all shut down,
An' everybody rush to town . . . "

(p.43).

Two more points: (i) Millington places the dialect version in quotes to signal (for him) its dramatic/conversational mode; (ii) at a reading of this poem by the author in 1979, he had removed the awkward standard English 'rutty' and imported from the dialect version the more natural 'full of holes'.

21

> Bow down my soul in worship very low
> And in the holy silences be lost
> Bow down before the marble Man of Woe,
> Bow down before the singing angel host . . .[22]

The only trouble is that McKay had 'trouble' with his syllables. His *Clarendon* vowels are very evident and he didn't always say 'the', but sometimes 'de'. And these elisions, the *sound* of them, subtly erode, somewhat, the classical pentametric of the sonnet . . .

Our second poet is George Campbell also of Jamaica. In 1945, Jamaica, after a long history of struggle, was granted by Britain the right to move toward self-government and independence with a new political Constitution and the formation of the People's National Party. George Campbell was very moved by and involved in these events and he wrote what I consider his finest poem :

> On this momentous night O God help us.
> With faith we now challenge our destiny.
> Tonight masses of men will shape, will hope,
> Will dream with us; so many years hang on
> Acceptance. Who is that knocking against
> The door? . . . is it you
> Looking for a destiny, or is it
> Noise of the storm?[23]

Now what you see here is a man becoming conscious of his nation. But when he comes to write his greatest poem, it is a Miltonic ode; or perhaps *because* he's writing his greatest poem, it must be given that kind of nobility.[24] And it is read here by our Milton of the Caribbean, George Lamming, our great organ

---

22. McKay, 'St Isaac's Church, Petrograd', first pub. in the *Survey Graphic* v.53, March 1, 1925, in *Selected poems* (New York 1953), p.84, *The passion of Claude McKay*, p.127 and read here by the author on *Anthology of Negro poets* (Folkways FL 9791, New York 1966).
23. George Campbell, 'On this night', *First poems* (Kingston 1945), p.67.
24. See *critical relativity*, n.21, above.

voice, a voice that he himself in his own book *The Pleasures of Exile* (1960) recognizes as one of the finest in English orature.[25] But the point is that from my perspective, George Campbell's ode, fittingly read by George Lamming, isn't giving us any unique element in terms of the Caribbean environment, though it is still a beautiful poem wonderfully read. (On tape : Lamming reading Campbell's poem . . .

> Must the horse rule the rider or the man
> The horse.
> Wind where cometh the fine technique
> Of rule passing through me ? My hands wet with
> The soil and I knowing my world

. . . followed by the opening of Beethoven's *Fifth Symphony*).[26]

The models are important here, you see. The McKay can be matched with Fauré, Campbell/Lamming with Beethoven. What follows next on the tape, however, is equally important because our *local* Beethoven employs a completely different model. I'm not saying his model is 'equal' to the *Fifth Symphony,* but it makes a similar statement, and it gets us into what

25. "I can read verse much better than most English poets alive. That is a fact. And I read it [at the ICA, London] exactly as I would have done in the West Indies. After all, it was my poem. I had made it. It was my own trumpet; and I knew the keys. If I were afraid to blow it, whom would I expect to do it for me? So I made a heaven of a *noise* [my italics] which is *characteristic of my voice and an ingredient of West Indian behaviour.* The result was an impression of authority. That's why they left me alone . . . "
   George Lamming, *The pleasures of exile* (London: Michael Joseph, 1960), pp.62 - 63.
26. The tape recordings used in this lecture were taken from a wide variety of sources : LPs, field recordings, copies from radio broadcasts, interviews etc. The Lamming recording is from one of our finest radio programmes, *New World of the Caribbean,* a series sponsored by Bookers of Guyana and broadcast on Radio Guyana in 1955/56. It was conceived of and written by Lamming and Wilson Harris and produced for radio by Rafiq Khan. The Lamming reading of Campbell's poem had as background the theme music of the entire series, Dvorak's *New World Symphony.*

I now consider the nation or native language. Big Yout's sound poem, 'Salaman Agunday' begins with a scream (on tape : Big Yout's 'Screamin'' target'/'Salaman Agunday' from the LP *Screamin' target*, Kingston c.1972) followed by the bass-based reggae-canter of downbeat on the first 'syllable' of the first and second bars, followed by a syncopation on the third third, followed by full offbeat/downbeats on the fourth :

The other model that we have and that we have always had in the Caribbean, as I've said before, is the calypso, and we are going to hear now the Mighty Sparrow singing a *kaiso* which came out in the early sixties. It marked, in fact, the first major change in consciousness that we all shared. And Sparrow made a criticism of all that I and Dennis have been saying about the educational system. In 'Dan is the Man in the Van' he says that the education we got from England has really made us idiots because all of those things that we had to read about—Robin Hood, King Alfred and the Cakes, King Arthur and the Knights of the Round Table—all of these things really haven't given us anything but empty words. And he did it in the calypso form. And you should hear the rhyme-scheme of this poem. He is rhyming on 'n's' and 'l's' and he is creating a cluster of syllables and a counterpoint between voice and orchestra, between individual and community, within the formal notion of 'call and response', which becomes typical of our nation in the revolution.

(Solo)   According to de education you get when you small
You(ll) grow up wi(th) true ambition an respec for one an all
But in *my* days in school they teach me like a fool
THE THINGS THEY TEACH ME A
    SHOULDA BEEN A BLOCK-HEADED
    MULE

---

27. 'Salaman Agunday' from *Screaming target* juxtaposed, on tape, with title tune.

24

(Chorus)   *Pussy has finish his work long ago*
            An now he restin an ting
            Solomon Agundy was born on a MunDEE
            DE ASS IN DE LION SKIN ...[28]

I could bring you a book, *The Royal Reader*, or the one re-
ferred to by Sparrow, *Nelson's West Indian Reader* by J. O.
Cutteridge, that we had to learn at school by heart, which con-
tained phrases like : 'the cow jumped over the moon', 'ding dong
bell, pussy in the well', 'Twisty & Twirly were two screws' and
so on. I mean, that was our beginning of an understanding of
literature. 'Literature' started (*startled*, really) literally at that
level, with that kind of model. It was all we had. The problem of
transcending this is what I am talking about now.

5

A more complex form by Sparrow is this next poem, 'Ten to
One is Murder'. Now it's interesting how this goes, because
Sparrow had been accused of shooting someone on the eve of
Carnival, just before Lent. (Kaiso and Carnival are two of our
great folk expressions.) Now Sparrow apparently shot someone,
but because of the popular nature of the calypsonian, he was
able to defend himself long before he got into court by creating
the scenario for the reason why he shot the man. He shot the
man, he says, because for no reason at all, ten angry men sud-
denly appear one night, surround him, and started throwing
stones. The one in front was a very good pelter, and he didn't
know what to do. He couldn't even find shelter. So he ran and
ran and ran until finally he remembered that he had a gun (a
wedger) in his pocket. He was forced to take it out and shoot
pow pow pow and the crowd start to scatter. As a result he had
the community on his side before the trial even started. But even

---

28. The Mighty Sparrow [Slinger Francisco], 'Dan is the man in the van',
    from an EP recording (1963). The fourth line of each quatrain,
    shouted by Sparrow on this recording, represents the 'response' part of
    this form and is sometimes sung by chorus and/or audience. For
    text of this kaiso, see *One hundred and twenty calypsoes to remember
    ... by the Mighty Sparrow* (Port of Spain 1963), p.86.

25

if he hadn't written the song, he would have had the community on his side because here you have a folk poet; and folk poets are the spokesmen whose whole concern is to express the experience of the people rather than the experiences of the elite. But here is 'Ten to One is Murder'. Each slash-phrase is an impressionistic brush-stroke :

> About ten in de night on de fifth of October
> *Ten to One is Murder!*
> Way down Henry Street, up by H. G. M. Walker
> *Ten to One is Murder!*
> Well de leader of de gang was a hot like a pepperrr
> *Ten to One is Murder!*
> An every man in de gang had a white-handle razorrr
> *Ten to One is Murder!*
> They say ah push a gal from Grenada
> *Ten to One is Murder! ...*

Now that is dramatic monologue which because of its call-and-response structure (in addition, of course, to its own intrinsic drama) is capable of extension on stage. There is in fact a 'tent' form known as calypso drama, which calls upon Trinidadian nation-forms like *grand charge, picong, robber talk,* and so on, which Sparrow is in fact consciously using in this calypso and which some of the younger Trinidadian *nation* poets like Malik, Questel and Christopher Laird, for example, are bringing into play in their poetry.

> Man a start to sweat. Man a soakin wet
> Mama so much threat : that's a night a can never
>   forget
> *Ten to One is Murder! ..."*

Next we have the poet who has been writing *nation* all her life and who, because of that, has been ignored until recently; the poet Louise Bennett (Miss Lou) of Jamaica. Now this is very interesting because she is middle class and 'middle class' means

---

29. Sparrow 'Ten to one is Murder', EP recording (Port of Spain 1960), text in *One hundred and twenty calypsoes,* p.37.

'brown',[30] urban/'respectable' and 'standard English' and 'the snow was falling in the canefields'. It certainly doesn't mean an entrenched economic/political position, as in Europe. For instance, Miss Lou's mother's and Miss Lou's own upbringing was 'rural St Mary':[31] hence the Honourable Louise's natural and rightful knowledge of the folk, though it was not until the post-independence seventies that she was officially—as distinct from popularly—recognized and given the highest honours—including the right to the title of Honourable. But one is supposed, as V. S. Naipaul once said at a memorable Writers Conference in Jamaica,[32] *to graduate out of these things;* therefore there is no reason why Louise should have persisted with Anancy and Auntie Roachie and *boonoonoonoos* an *parangles* an *ting,* when she could have opted for 'And how are you today': the teeth and lips tight and closed around the mailed fist of a smile. But her instincts were that she should use the language of her people. The consequence was that for years (since c.1936)[33] she performed her work in crowded village halls across the island, and until 1945[34] could get nothing accepted by *The Gleaner,* the island's largest, oldest (estab. 1834) and often only newspaper, and at that time (still is, to a large extent) a budding writer's only outlet. (Claude McKay had published in Kingston, including *The Gleaner* in 1912 but he had had an influential white sponsor, the Englishman Walter Jekyll, compiler of *Jamaican song*

30. For the role of colour in the Caribbean, see Fernando Henriques, *Family and colour in Jamaica* (London 1953).

31. See the (in progress) Ph.D. dissertation by Mary Jane Hewitt (Dept of English/History, UWI, Mona) on Louise Bennett and Zora Neale Hurston as 'cultural conservators'.

32. ACLALS (Association of Commonwealth Lit. & Lang. Societies) Conference held at the UWI, Mona, Jamaica, in January 1971; see my 'The love axe/1: developing a Caribbean aesthetic' in *Speaking Black: essays in the criticism of African, Caribbean, and Black American literature,* ed. Houston A. Baker, Jr (Cornell Univ. Press, 1976), *Bim* 61-63 (1977-78); and, in detail, in a book of the same title, forthcoming New Beacon Books, London.

33. Hewitt, loc. cit.

34. Hewitt's information is that Louise Bennett began to write for *The Gleaner* in 1942—two years after that company had, in fact, printed her first book of poetry, *Dialect verses* (1940).

and story [1907])."³⁵ And although by 1962 she had already pub-
lished nine books, she does not appear among the poets in the
Independence Anthology of Jamaican Poetry but is at the back
of the book, like an afterthought if not an embarrassment, under
'Miscellaneous'. She could not be accepted, even at the moment
of Political Independence, as a poet. Though all this, as I say,
is dramatically altered now with the revolution of the late 60s,
her consciousness of this unfortunate situation remains where it
hurts most : *'I have been set apart by other creative writers a
long time ago because of the language I speak and work in . . .
From the beginning nobody recognized me as a writer'.*³⁶

I couldn't satisfactorily reproduce in print Miss Lou's 'Street
cries' played for the lecture from her LP *Miss Lou's Views.*³⁷
Here instead are two examples of her more 'formal' verse from
the book collection *Jamaica labrish* (Kingston 1966). Recordings
from which, Miss Lou informs me, should be available alongside

35. McKay's relationship with Jekyll is recorded in McKay's auto-
biography, *My green hills of Jamaica* (Kingston 1979), pp.65-72,
76-79. "Now is your chance as a native boy [to] put the Jamaican
dialect into literary language. I am sure that your poems will sell"
(p.67). Jekyll's *Jamaican song and story* was published by David
Nutt, London in 1907 and reprinted by Dover Publications, Inc.,
New York in 1966. For useful notes on Jekyll, see Cooper, *The
passion of Claude McKay*, pp.318-19.
Mary Jane Hewitt gives this account of McKay's influence on Louise
Bennett :

> It was during this period of high unemployment, labour unrest and
> Garveyism in the 1920s that Louise first saw Jamaican creole
> language in print. When she was about seven years of age, a
> teacher at Calabar School in Kingston (Miss Dukes), knowing
> the child was always telling her classmates Anancy stories, gave
> her a copy of Claude McKay's *Constab Ballads* (1912), saying,
> "Here are some verses a man wrote in the Jamaican talk. You must
> read some of them. They're very funny!" [Miss Lou] took the
> book home and showed it to her Grandma Mimi who liked the
> poems. Bibs [Louise] memorized some of them, but whenever
> she told someone she knew Claude McKay's *Constab Ballads*,
> they would respond with, "Oh, yes", and refer to his sonnets from
> *Songs of Jamaica* (also 1912).

Ms Hewitt is in error here in that McKay's sonnets do not appear
in print until *Spring in New Hampshire* (1920)—after he'd gone to
the USA. Both the 1912 books are in 'dialect'.
36. Bennett, *Caribbean Quarterly,* 4: 1&2 (March-June 1968), p.98.
37. Federal 204, Federal Records, Kingston ?1967.

the revised edition of *Labrish* quite soon."[38] First, 'Pedestrian crosses':

> If a cross yuh dah-cross,
> Beg yuh cross mek me pass.
> Dem yah crossin' is crosses yuh know!
> Koo de line! Yuh noh se
> Cyar an truck backa me?
> Hear dah hoganeer one deh dah-blow!
>
> Missis, walk fas' an cross!
> Pickney, cross mek me pass!
> Lady, galang an mine yuh business!
> Ole man mek up yuh mine
> Walk between dem white line!
> Wat a crosses dem crossin yah is!
> . . .
> De crossin a-stop we from pass mek dem cross,
> But nutten dah-stop dem from cross mek we pass,
> Dem yah crossin is crosses fe true![39]

And 'Dutty tough' begins

> Sun a-shine but tings noh bright,
> Doah pot a-bwile, bickle noh nuff,
> River flood but water scarce yaw,
> Rain a-fall but dutty tuff!

And ends on this note of social commentary:

> De price o' bread gan up so high
> Dat we haffe agree,
> Fe cut we y'eye pon bread an all
> Tun dumplin refugee!

---

38. Personal communication, Louise Bennett Coverley, 25 September 1978.
39. Louise Bennett, 'Pedestrian crosses', *Jamaica labrish* [Kingston] 1966. p.74.

An all dem mawga smaddy weh
Dah-gwan like fat is sin,
All dem deh weh dah-fas' wid me,
Ah lef dem to dumplin!

Sun a-shine an pot a-bwile, but
Ting noh bright, bickle noh nuff!
Rain a-fall, river dah-flood, but
Wata scarce an dutty tuff!⁴⁰

6

These are the models that we have, and I could give you much
more complex examples than the ones you have so far heard.
What I am going to do now, however, since there is a constraint
on time for this session, is give you an idea of how the 'main-
stream' anglophone Caribbean poets reached the stage signalled
by Miss Lou.

The 'mainstream' poets who were moving from standard
English to nation language were influenced basically, I think,
(again the models are important) by T. S. Eliot. What T. S.
Eliot did for Caribbean poetry and Caribbean literature was to
introduce the notion of the speaking voice, the conversational
tone.⁴¹ That is what really attracted us to Eliot. And you can see
how the Caribbean poets introduced here have been influenced

40. Bennett, 'Dutty tough', *Labrish*, pp.120-121. The tyranny of the
pentametre can be seen/heard quite clearly here, although Miss Lou
erodes and transforms this with the sound of her language. Its
riddim sets up a counterpoint *against* the pentametre: "River flood
but water scarce/yaw"; "Yuh noh se/Cyar an truck *backa me*". The
'Africanisms' (*koo de, galang, yah, yaw, noh nuff, deh dah-blow* and
fe, for example) carry this even further, crystallising in brilliant roots
images such as "like fat is sin" and "tun dumplin refugee", which
not only has its 'English' meaning, but its folk-speech underdrone of
African sound-words for food: *tun, tum, tuntum* and *fungee*. A
whole essay could (and should) be written on the phonemic structure
of nation language and how this relates to syntax and prosody, in
addition to the historical and critical/comparative approaches hinted
at in note 21 of this study.
41. For those who really made the breakthrough, it was Eliot's actual
voice — or rather his recorded voice, property of the British
Council — reading 'Preludes', 'The love song of J. Alfred Prufrock',

30

by him, although they eventually went on to become part of their own environmental expression.

The first poet (writing in the 1940s) is a magistrate and historian from Barbados, H. A. Vaughan, and he is reading a sonnet called 'For certain demogogues'. It is a 'standard English' poem except for a passage toward the end when the image of 'blackbirds' appears. Here, suddenly for the first time and rare in Vaughan's poetry, he imitates the sound and the motion, the movement of the hopping of these peculiar birds and gets this into his poetry, which becomes one of the first and early stages of nation language : *mimesis*. In fact, had I not *heard* this poem, I might never have 'recognized' it.

> 'We *love* the people, sir !' You do ?
> You ought to ! nay, indeed, you must
> Shouting their needs has brought a new
> Elation to your fickle dust
>
> . . .
>
> You prey, but not like *beasts* of prey;
> The cobblers fly too far to be
> Your emblem; in a higgling way
> You have a place in history;

The Waste Land and the *Four Quartets* — not the texts — which turned us on. In that dry deadpan delivery, the riddims of St Louis (though we didn't know the source then) were stark and clear for those of us who at the same time were listening to the dislocations of Bird, Dizzy and Klook. And it is interesting that on the whole, the Establishment couldn't stand Eliot's voice—far less jazz! Eliot himself, in the sleeve note to *Four Quartets* (HMV CLP 1115, n.d.) says: "What a recording of a poem by its author can and should preserve, is the way that poem sounded to the author when he had finished it. The disposition of lines on the page, and the punctuation (which includes the *absence* of punctuation marks . . .) can never give an exact notation of the author's metric. The chief value of the author's record . . . is a guide to the *rhythms*" [my italics]. Another influence must have been the voice of John Arlott, the BBC test cricket commentator, who stunned, amazed and transported us with his natural, *riddmic* and *image*-laden tropes, in its revolutionary Hampshire burr, at a time when BBC meant Empire and Loyal Models and Our Masters Voice: and cricket, especially against England, was the national war-game, our colonial occasion for communal catharsis. Not only was Arlott 'good' (all our mimics tried to imitate him) but he subverted the Establishment with the way and where he spoke: like Eliot, like jazz . . .

31

Like blackbirds in their shiny coats
Prinking and lifting spry, proud feet,
Bickering and picking sodden oats
From horses' offal in the street.[42]

Now we must also hear from Frank Collymore, who is[43] a schoolmaster and editor of the magazine *Bim* that I mentioned earlier. Here is the conversational tone of the early 50s. He is talking about going back to school and the materialist dangers of scholastic education, continuing the theme in fact being raised by Dennis Brutus' lecture and Sparrow's calypso and Big Yout's 'Salaman Agundy' but getting it all into a wonderfully achieved style and tone. There is however, no nation language as such here; no unique element similar to Vaughan's 'blackbirds', for instance. But the *conversational mode* can have a corrosive effect on the tyranny of the pentameter :

In a couple of weeks' time school will reopen
    If not with a flourish of trumpets at least with a shout
From the several hundred boys gathered together in the building,
    And though a few perhaps may wonder what it's all about . . .
This fuss of education, I mean . . . their parents and the others
    Who have to fit the bill of books and shoes
Will be prouder than ever that their young are well on the road
    To knowledge—not that they'll be caring particularly who's
Going to dish out the stuff, or even what it is for that matter,
    Only the platters have got to be picked clean,
And afterwards with the School Certificate nicely framed
    And the New Order hovering suspiciously near the scene !
French irregular verbs, quadratic equations,

---

42. H. A. Vaughan 'For certain demagogues', read by the author on *Poets of the West Indies reading their own works* (Caedmon TC 1379, New York 1971) from *Sandy Lane and other poems* (B'town 1945), *Caribbean voices II*, ed. John Figueroa (London 1970), pp.71-72. By *cobblers* Vaughan does not mean ye olde English shoemakers, but sea-birds. Vaughan's reading of the stanza italicized is especially interesting . . .

43. Colly (b.1893) died in July 1980, while this version of my talk was being prepared. I should like here to pay tribute to his warmth, kindness and humanity, and to his enormous contribution to Caribbean literature.

Maybe a century in the First Division . . . who knows?
And for those who can't take it all in by the prescribed method
There's a road to the brain through the backside by blows . . ."

Our third 'established' poet, John Figueroa, writing in the
late 60s, now begins to use nation language, but he uses it as a
very self-conscious and formal contrast to standard English, as
a reaction, no doubt, to the folk/nation rupture (I won't say
irruption, though some hoped that it was merely an *interruption*)
that had taken place in our poetry with the publication of *Rights
of passage* (London 1967) and the effects of the literary debate
that had taken place a few years before on the issue of 'literature
and dialect' (1965) when it was demonstrated for perhaps the
first time at last that a nation language poem could be 'serious'
and employ not only semantic but *sound* elements : in this case,
the sound-structure of Rastafarian drums and the 'Dry bones'
spiritual in 'Wings of a Dove' :

> Watch *dem* ship *dem*
> *come* to *town* dem
>
> full o' *silk* dem
> full o' *food* dem
>
> an' *dem* plane *dem*
> *come* to *groun'* dem
>
> full o' *flash* dem
> full o' *cash* dem
>
> silk *dem* food *dem*
> shoe *dem* wine *dem*
>
> date *dem* drink *dem*
> an consume *dem*

---

44. Frank Collymore, 'Voici la plume de mon oncle', *Collected poems*
(Bridgetown 1959), p.92; read by the author on *Poets of the West
Indies,* q.v.

This riddimic aspect of Caribbean nation language was to be
further extended in the late seventies by the Jamaican reggae/
dub poets Oku Onuora (Orlando Wong), Michael Smith (whom
we shall hear from later) and Linton Kwesi Johnson of Black
London in, for instance, 'Come wi goh dung deh' from his LP
Dread beat an blood :

>   de people demma fite
>   fe work dung deh
>   de people dem a fite
>   one annadda dung deh
>
>   de people demma fite
>   fe stay alive dung deh
>   de people demma fite
>   fe dem rites dung deh
>   . . .
>
>   soh come we goh dung deh
>   mek wi mek a stop dung deh
>   soh come wi goh dung deh
>   mek we forward dung deh
>   gonna ba16ttuppa ba6tuppa badituppa . . .
>
>   come wi goh dung deh ![46]

or, more complex,

---

45. Edward Kamau Brathwaite, 'Wings of a dove', *Rights of passage*
(London 1967), p.44. *The arrivants* (London 1973), p.45; read by the
author on Argo DA 101 (London 1969), Argo DA 1110 (London
1972). The literary debate took place at the UWI, Mona (1965) at a
Sunday Morning Seminar involving, among others, Errol Hill, Derek
Walcott, Mervyn Morris, Rex Nettleford and Edward Kamau Brath-
waite. Transcripts (were) available from the Radio Unit at Mona.

46. Linton Kwesi Johnson, 'Come wi goh dung deh', *Dread beat an
blood,* Virgin Records (London 1978), text in *Dread beat and blood*
(London 1975), p.49.

night number one was in BRIX/TON :
SOFRANO B sounn sys/tem

was a-beatin out a riddim/wid a fy*ah*,
commin doun his reggae-reggae wy*ah*;

it was a sounn shakin doun you spinal col/umn,
a bad music tearin up you *flesh*;
an th'rebels-dem start a-fightin,
th'yout dem jus tunn *wild*.

it's *war* amongst th' rebels :
mad/ness . . . mad/ness . . . *war* . . .[47]

so wid a flick
a de wrist
a jab an a stab

th' song of blades was *soun*/ded
th' bile of oppression was *vom*/ited
an two policemen *woun*/ded

*r*ighteous *r*ighteous *war*[48]

But nation language isn't confined, as you must have recognized by now, to rhythmic variations. Miss Lou follows the traditional Scots tune very nicely thank you with her 'Every secky got him jeggeh/Every puppy got him flea'; while I got pretty close to Bajan country speech (free cadence and vocabulary) in 'The Dust', also from *Rights of passage*, where some women are recalling a volcanic eruption in another island :

. . . Some say
is in one o' dem islands away

where they language tie-tongue
an' to hear them speak so
in they St Lucia patois

47. Linton Kwesi Johnson, 'Five nights of bleedin' from the LP *Dread beat an blood,* and the book. p.15, as cited above.
48. ibid.

is as if they cahn unnerstan'

a single word o' English.
But uh doan really know. All uh know
is that one day suddenly so
this mountain leggo one *brugg-a-lung-go*

whole bloody back side
o' this hill like it blow
off like they blastin' stones
in de quarry.

Rocks big as you cow pen hois'
in de air as if they was one
set o' shingles. That noise,
Jesus Chrise, mussa rain down

splinter an' spark
as if it was Con-
federation.[49]

But the roots and underground link to all these emerging
forces was the now almost legendary Rastafarian poet, Bongo
Jerry, whose revolutionary mis/use of Babylonian English was
practically apocalyptic :

MABRAK

Lightning
is the future brightening,
for last year man learn
how to use black eyes.
(wise !)

MABRAK :
                NEWSFLASH !
'Babylon plans crash'

49. Edward Kamau Brathwaite, 'The dust', *Rights*, pp.66-67, *The arrivants*,
    pp.65-66, read here on Argo 102 or 1111. (The Argo recording is on
    two LPs).

Thunder interrupt their programme to
announce :

BLACK ELECTRIC STORM

                    IS HERE

How long you feel 'fair to fine'
(WHITE) would last?

How long in darkness
     when out of BLACK
     come forth LIGHT?

       ....

MABRAK is righting the wrongs and brain-whitening...
Not just by washing out the straightening and wearing
    dashiki t'ing

MOSTOFTHESTRAIGHTENINGISINTHE
    TONGUE—so . . .

Save the YOUNG
from the language that MEN teach,
the doctrine Pope preach
skin bleach . . .

     MAN must use MEN language
     to carry dis message :

SILENCE BABEL TONGUES : recall and
recollect BLACK SPEECH[50]

---

50. Bongo Jerry, *Savacou* 3/4 (Dec 1970/March 1971), pp.13-15. At the
Harvard lecture, a tape recording of Bongo Jerry reading 'Mabrak',
with *funde* and *repeater* drums, at a Rasta *grounnation* (Kingston
1969) was used. Also Jerry's 'slide-trombone' tribute to Don Drum-
mond, Bob Marley's musical and spiritual ancestor, from Dermott
Hussey's (JBC Radio 1969, 1980) *Requiem for Don Drummond*.
The influence of this *roots underground* is described in my 'Love
axe/1' (p.32).

Now Figueroa's nation language, and that of many other of the established poets who followed, was very likely a reaction to (and against) all this. But the difference at this stage between Figueroa/mainstream and the natives (the *cultural gorillas*) per se, was that while for the natives nation language informs the very shape and spirit of their poems, for Figueroa in 'Portrait of a Woman', for instance, the control and narrative, the 'classical', even *Prosperian element*—the *most* part of the poem—is in *English*. The marginal bit, that of the voice and status of the domestic helper, *the house slave,* Caliban's sister, is in nation but a nation still sticky and wet with the interposition of dialect; though Figueroa might claim that the glory of Caribbean English is that it has a wide range of resources and we should use them all. In any case, Figueroa, when all is said and done, finally sets up a most memorable cross-rhythm :

> Firmly, sweetly
> refusing . . .

> Tall for seventeen fit
> for a tumble

>> ('*A guess hard time*
>> *tek er*') she said
>> referring to
>> her mother's misfortune
>> (Her strict mother whose
>> three men had left
>> her holding five pledges to fortune)

> She came easily into
> my arms
> refusing only to kiss
>> ('*any familiarity an*
>> *we stop right now*')

> Dixerat—as lacrymae rerum used to say.
> She's in the public domain
> she's lost her patent rights . . .

'You have bad min'
doan tell nobody
doan tell nobody
doan mek me do it
    mek mi
doan mek me do it
    mek mi
     lawd!
You see I intend to be a nurse'
No need to apologise
(*Lawd it sweet!*)
'But if you try to kiss
me I will scream.'[51]

---

51. John Figueroa, 'Portrait of a woman', *Savacou* 3/4 (Dec 1970/
March 1971), pp.138-39, *Ignoring hurts* (Washington, D.C., 1976),
pp.98-99, my italics; read by the author on *Poets of the West Indies*.
Figueroa's *dialect* (not *nation*) position in the debate perhaps best
expresses itself in this poem (in the *Ambit* 91 (1982) anthology)
'Problems of a writer who does not Quite . . . /For: Derek Walcott,
his brother Roddy, his mother Alix and After reading Helen Vendler's
Review of Walcott in The New York Review of Books' (pp. 84-85):

    Roddy broder, teacher Alix son,
    Bwoy, you no hear wa de lady say?
    Watch dis pentemeter ting, man.
    Dat is white people play!

    Wha de hell yu read Homer—
    A so him name?—fa!
    Yu his from the horal tradition
    And must deal wid calypso and reggae na!

    Mek I hadvise yu boy
    If yu trouble white people toy
    (Especially as yu win big prize an t'ing)
    Yu arse goin swing

    Like metronome, yu'd say,
    But a black bwoy should play
    Widout dem mechanical aids
    Full of rydhm like all true spades.

    (Eh eh a since when yu tun black?
    Yu note-book does say yu never did notice
    Whedr the sore was black or white dat wear de poultice,
    But de lady slap 'black experience' in yu back!)

Next Derek Walcott, the Caribbean's most accomplished poet/playwright, with a poem about a little night-violence in New York called 'Blues', which is not a blues at all; it doesn't have that form. But it is a wonderfully speech-textured piece, giving *form* to Collymore's conversational style. And the blues is there in Walcott's *voice*. You will hear in his reading (the print/ text can't reveal these things) the sound of Don Drummond's trombone . . .

> Those five or six young guys
> hunched on the stoop
> that oven-hot summer night
> whistled me over. Nice
> and friendly. So I stop.
> Macdougal or Christopher
> Street in chains of light . . ."

See what dat pentameter an' ESSAY do
To yu bwoy! Long time I school yu
To break
    up yu
Lines
    Lines
        Lines
Like dat black writer Poe, black like his raven

Bruck it
    up
Man
    Bruck it up man
Bruck it
    up
       man   an' wid de drums
                   de drums

De tinti
    nab   u
            la
tion of de drums, de drums
Black bwoy black bwoy
                black
Bwoy . . .

52. Derek Walcott, 'Blues', *The gulf and other poems* (London 1969), p.34; (New York 1970), p.67; read by the author on *Poetry International '69* (Argo, London 1970). In my presentation, Walcott's reading was followed by Don Drummond's 'Green Island' solo (Kingston c.1966).

Don Drummond, Jamaican ghetto/culture hero of the fifties and early sixties, was a jazz musician of genius (I would compare him with J. J. Johnson), who was at the same time one of the originators of *ska,* the native sound at the yardway of the cultural revolution that would lead eventually to Bob Marley, reggae and *The Harder They Come.*[53] It is a connection of Caribbean and Harlem/New Orleans which Buddy Bolden and Congo Square knew about, which McKay was to carry forward and which, in this poem, among some others (see especially *The Gulf*) Derek Walcott continues. And it is this connection which brings in the influence of Langston Hughes for instance, and Imamu Baraka for instance, and Sonia Sanchez for instance, and Miles Davis, which further erodes the pentameter . . .

My face smashed in, my bloody mug
pouring, my olive-branch jacket saved
from cuts and tears,
I crawled four flights upstairs . . .

I
remember a few watchers waved
loudly, and one kid's mother shouting
like 'Jackie' or 'Terry',
'Now that's enough!'
It's nothing really.
They don't get enough love.

---

53. The premier of the Jimmy Cliff roots/reggae film, *The harder they come* (Kingston 1972) marked a dislocation in the socio-colonial pentameter, in the same way that its music and its stars and their *style,* marked a revolution in the hierarchical structure in the arts of the Caribbean. At the premier, the traditional 'order of service' was reversed. Instead of the elite, from their cars moving (complimentary) into the Carib Cinema watched by the poor and admiring multitude, the multitude took over—the car park, the steps, the barred gates, the magical lantern itself—and demanded that they see what they had wrought. 'For the first time at last' it was the people (the raw material) not the 'critics', who decided the criteria of praise, the measure and ground of qualification; 'for the first time at last', a local face, a native ikon, a nation language voice was hero. In this small corner of our world, a revolution as significant as Emancipation.

You know they wouldn't kill
you. Just playing rough
like young America will.
Still, it taught me something
about love. If it's so tough,
forget it.[54]

Today, we have a very confident movement of nation lan-
guage. In fact, it is inconceivable that any Caribbean poet writ-
ing today is not going to be influenced by this submerged/emerg-
ing culture. And it is obvious now to most Caribbean writers, I
would say, except perhaps some of the most 'exiled',[55] (and there
are less and less of them!) that one has to communicate with
the audience. No one is going to assert that a poet cannot live
in his ivory tower, or that a poet cannot be an 'individual'—all
that we have been through already. But the point is that for the
needs of the kind of emerging society that I am defending—for
the people who have to recite 'The boy/stood on/the burn/ing
deck' for so long, who are unable to express the power of the
hurricane in the way that they write their words—at last, our
poets, today, are recognizing that it is essential that they use
the resources which have always been there, but which have
been denied to them—and which they have sometimes them-
selves denied.[56]

54. Walcott, 'Blues'. After this comes 'The schooner Flight', read by the
author in Port of Spain 1978, text in *Trinidad & Tobago Review*,
(May 1978), *The star apple kingdom* (New York 1979).

55. Exile is the first significant feature of anglophone Caribbean writing:
the need—or the imagined need—to emigrate to metropolitan centres
in order to exist as writers. Our native literature begins with McKay
the exile (see *Home to Harlem*, New York 1928) and is ending its
first phase with George Lamming (*The pleasures of exile*, London
1960) and V.S. Naipaul (see *Newsweek*, August 18, 1980).

56. In 'The love axe/1' (see n.32, above) I have gone at some detail into
the context of this assertion.

7

I shall end with the violet and red extremes of the spectrum.
Here, first, is *fundamental nation,* the language of a *kumina*
queen, with its *kikongo* base. Again, although there is no ques-
tion about the beauty and power of Miss Queenie's language
and images: she is, after all, priestess, prophet and symbolist:
without hearing her *(seeing* her of course completes the experi-
ence because then you would know how she uses her eyes, her
mouth, her whole face; how her arms encircle and reject; how
her fingers can become water or spear); but without hearing her,
you would miss the dynamics of the narrative: the blue notes of
that voice; its whispers and pauses and repetitions and stutters
and eleisons; its high pitch emphases and its low fall trails; and
that hoarse quality which I suppose you know from Nina
Simone. With Miss Queenie, we are in the very ancient dawn of
nation language and to be able to come to terms with oral litera-
ture at all, our critics must be able to understand the complex
forces that have led to this classical expression . . .

> One day . . .
> a remember one day a faen some lillies . . .
> an a plant de lillies-dem in row
> an one Sunday mornin when a wake . . .
> all de lillies blow . . .
> *seven* lillies an de seven a dem blow . . .
>
> an a *leave* . . .
> an guh dung in de gully bottom . . .
> to go an pick some quoquonut
> an when a go
> a see a cottn tree an a juss *fell* right down . . .
> at de cottn tree root . . .
>
> . . .

in de night
in de cottn tree comin like it hollooow
an hi hinside there
an you have some grave arounn dat cottn tree
right rounn it
some *tombs* . . .

but dose is
some hol-time Hafrican
yu unnerstann . . . ?

well dose tombs arounn de cottn tree . . .
an hi inside de cottn tree lay down
an a night-time a sih de cotton tree *light* hup wit
    cyandles an . . .
a restin now
put me an *dis* way an sleepin . . .

an a honly hear a likkle *vice*
come to mih
an dem talkin to mih
but dose tings is spirit talkin to mih . . .
an dem speakin to me now
an seh now . . .

'Is a likkle *nice* likkle chile
an oo gwine get im right up now . . .
in de hafrican worl . . .
because you brains
you will *take* someting . . .
so derefore . . .
we gine to *teach* you someting . . .'

Well de *firs* ting dat dem teach me is
s'wikkidi . . .

s'wikkidi lango
which is sugar an water . . .

44

sih?
an dem teach me dat . . .

an dem teach me m'praey-ers . . .
which is . . .

Kwale kwale n'den den de
Belo ko lo mawa kisalaya

Pem legele
Len legele

Luwi za'kwe n'da'kwe so
Be'lam m'pese m'bambe

which is de same Hour Fader's Praeyer . . ."

Michael Smith (b. Kingston 1954) is such an intransigent
sound-poet that he's not concerned with written script at all. He
'publishes', like a calypsonian, at his public poetry readings at
Zinc Fence Theatre or School of Drama auditorium or like the
early Louise Bennett, in all the large or little places throughout
Jamaica where he's constantly invited to appear. But whereas it
was years before Louise was 'recognized', Smith is a pop star like
Oku Onuora and Paul Keens-Douglas, two other very popular
sound-poets, who have actually appeared, in performance with
Marley and Tosh and Sparrow; while the sound/poems of Lin-
ton Kwesi Johnson are on the charts in Britain." For these in-
heritors of the revolution, nation-language is no longer anything

57. Imogene Elizabeth Kennedy (Miss Queenie), tape recorded con-
    versation with Maureen Warner Lewis and Monica Schuler, King-
    ston, June 1971. See Brathwaite and Warner Lewis, n.12, above.
58. Both Kwesi Johnson's LPs to date (*Dread beat an blood* 1978,
    Bass culture 1980) have been on the British reggae charts. *Bass
    culture* was at No. 3 in June 1980 (see *Black Music and Jazz Review,*
    June 1980, p.12). Oku Onuora has performed with Bob Marley,
    Keens-Douglas with The Mighty Sparrow *and* with Miss Lou, Brath-
    waite with the Mystic Revelation of Rastafari and Light of Saba,
    Michael Smith with Saba (*Word Sound,* Kingston 1978) and Malik
    (Trinidad) has presented several elaborate concerts with his own
    musicians. For more on these developments, see Brathwaite, 'Explo-
    sions in Caribbean "sound poetry",' *Caribbean Contact* (Oct. 1978);
    Jamaica Daily News 6 Oct 1978.

to argue about or experiment with; it is their classical norm and comes out of the same experience as the music of contemporary popular song : using the same riddims, the same voice-spreads, syllable clusters, blue notes, ostinado, syncopation and pauses; with, in Smith's case, a quite remarkable voice and breath control, accompanied by a decorative S90 *noise* (the S90 is an admired Japanese motorbike) which after a time becomes part of the sound-structure[59] and meaning of the poem. On the page, Smith's *Lawwwwwwwwwd* is the S90. He also, like Big Yout and Sparrow and Miss Lou, uses ring-game refrain and proverb as reverb/eration with again amen and amen to the pentameter/computer

> *Mi sey mi cyaan believe it*
> *mi sey mi cyaan believe it*
>
> room dem a rent
> mi apply widin
> but as mi go in
> cockroach an scarpian also come in
>
> *an mi cyaan believe it*
>
> one likkle bwoy come blow im orn
> an mi look pan im wid scorn
> an mi realize ow mi fine bwoy pickney
> was a victim a de trix
> dem kall partisan pally-trix

59. The concept of *noise* ('sonority contrasts') as part of the music of oral tradition has pervaded (for several reasons) this presentation. I am indebted to Kwabena Nketia for clarifying for me the idea. (See also his *The music of Africa* (London 1975), esp. pp.67-138, on Instrumental Resources). Noise is that decorative energy that invests the nation performance. Unnecessary but without which not enough. Whistles, grater, scraper, shak-shak, shekesheke, wood block, gong gong, the cheng-cheng of the steel band, the buzz of the banjo or cymbal, the grrill of the guitar, vibrato of voice, sax, sound-system, the long roll of the drum until it becomes thunder, Coltrane's sheets of sound, Pharoah Sanders' honks and cries, onomatopoeia, congregational kinesis . . . See also Shake Keane's LP *That's the noise* ACL 1219 (London 1966). One of the poems that perhaps best employs this kind of resource is my 'Nametracks' in *Mother Poem* (London 1977), pp.56-64.

an mi ban mi belly an mi baaal
an mi ban mi belly an mi baaal
Lawwwwwd
my cyaaan believe it

Mi dawta bwoyfren name is sailor
an im pass trew de port like a ship

more gran pickney fi feed
but de whole a wi need
wat a night wat a plight an we cyaan get a bite/mi life
   is a stiff fite
an mi cyaaan believe it . . .

> *Hi bwoy*
> yes mam
> *Hi bwoy*
> yes mam
> *Yu clean up de dwag shit?*
> yes mam
> *an mi cyaaan believe it*

Doris a moder a four
get a wuk as a domestic
boss man move in
an baps si sicai she pregnant again
baps si sicai an she pregnant again
an mi cyaaan believe it . . .

lawwwwwwwwwd . . .

but mi know yu believe it
lawwwwwwwwwwwwwwwd
mi know you believe it . . ."

60. Michael Smith, 'Mi cyaaan believe it', *Word Sound* (Light of Saba, Kingston 1978) with written version from draft by Smith and transcription by Brathwaite in Brathwaite (ed.), *New poets from Jamaica* (Savacou 14/15, Mona 1979), pp.84-86.

8

A full presentation of nation language would of course include more traditional (ancestral/oral) material than I have done (shango, *anansesem*, Spiritual (Aladura) Baptist services, groun-nations, yard theatres, ring games, tea-meeting speeches etc: in fact, I've included none of these here), in addition to the extended performances by Malik, Paul Keens-Douglas and the Barbados Writers Workshop, among others. In addition to the influence of Caribbean music on Caribbean poetry, there has also

---

Since these notes were written (1981), the three leading Jamaican nation language (dub/reggae) poets: Mutabaraka, Oku Onuora and Michael Smith have bloomed from strength to strength. Apart from increasing local recognition and influence, they have all made immensely successful metropolitan tour/impacts: Muta in the USA, Oku and Smith in the UK and Europe; they each have published at least one LP (plus, in the case of Oku and Muta, several 'singles') and these discs have been receiving wide airplay in Jamaica and all the countries they have visited. I was present (and participating) in the poetry reading at the First International Book Fair of Radical Black and Third World Books held in London in April 1982 when Oku and especially Mickey Smith were received into the bosom (I can find no better expression) of that tremendous audience of our people; and I was later able to get a sound copy of the BBC TV special on Michael Smith which contained, along with context shots and poetry of Jamdung and Brixton, a conversation with Smith and C. L. R. James. On 19 August 1983 the following item appeared in Kingston's *Daily Gleaner:*

> One of the country's leading 'dub' poets (those who recite poetry to reggae rhythm), Michael Smith, 29, of Golden Spring, St Andrew, was killed on Wednesday morning, August 17, in the neighbouring area of Stony Hill, when he was hit on the head by a stone thrown by one of three men who had attacked him . . .
>
> The police reported that Smith was on the Stony Hill Road near the old St. Jude's Church when he was set upon by the men. Struck on the head, he fell to the ground.
>
> He was taken to the clinic at Stony Hill by a passing motorist and then to the Kingston Public Hospital but by that time he had died. His attackers fled before the arrival of the police . . .
>
> He was to leave the island next month for engagements in the United Kingdom, where he had performed before . . .

Rumours persist that his killing was a flash of that same political violence which his work so eloquently decried.

been jazz, for example,[61] and the wonderful speech rhythm effects being achieved in a more formal context by Morris, Scott and Derek Walcott, among others

> O so yu is Walcott?
> You is Roddy brother?
> Teacher Alix son?[62]

Indeed, since this *History* was first conceived and presented at Carifesta 76 in Jamaica, there has been such a liberation of the voice in Caribbean poetry, that nation-language has become not the exception but almost the rule, except that because of its organic, its person-centred, fluid/tidal rather than ideal/structured nature, that word won't really be appropriate in this context. What we need, now, to go along with the liberation, is a re-orientation of criticism, an aesthetic, that will help us to re-define our current pseudo-classical notions of literature. In the same way that we have come to accept the idea (and reality) of Caribbean speech as continuum : ancestral through creole to national and international forms, so must we begin to be able to recognize and accept the similarly remarkable range of literary expression within the Caribbean and throughout Plantation America. To confine our definitions of literature to written texts in a culture that remains ital in most of its people proceedings, is as limiting as its opposite : trying to define Caribbean literature as essentially orature—like eating avocado without its likkle salt.

But we are dealing, too, with far more than sacred text or resonanting tape. The detonations within Caribbean sound-poetry have imploded us into new shapes and consciousness of ourselves, so that suddenly a *Dictionary of Caribbean English* is no longer list but life. Bob Marley and Oku's riddmic words become Authorities for linguists. The hidden world and proverb and conundrum (drum) reconquer the curriculum and make

61. See Brathwaite, 'Jazz and the West Indian novel', loc.cit., n.12. For Caribbean jazz poems, see Brathwaite's 'Jazz Poems' in *Kyk-over-al* 27(Dec 1960), pp.83-86, with versions in *Other exiles* (1975), pp.12-16; and some of the poems in Anthony McNeill's *Credences at the altar of cloud* (Kingston 1979), esp. influenced by McCoy Tyner.
62. Derek Walcott, 'Sainte Lucie', *Sea Grapes* (London 1976), p.46.

once more neglected Gran an expert on the culture. The word becomes a pebble stone or bomb and dub makes sense (or non-senseness) of politics demanding of it life not death, community not aardvark, new world to make new words and we to over-stand how modern ancient is. Like in this nation-language poem that doesn't even have to use a verb of nation . . .

> Strange   my writing to you
> Can I say a cliché
> Never thought I would see the day when you would cut
> me   glimpsed you in   should have said at   should
> have said near   a bank one day; smiled; waved; and
> you cut me
> Catherine   name from the north
> . . .
> Catherine   name like a fir
> The leaves turn with a fine cadence   The dancers touch
> hands under the elms
> . . .
> I cry to the stones because I am lonely, the girl said to the
> dark
> Perhaps if I look through this file I will find her charred
> letter
> Catherine and Natalie, moving
> The most beauteous virgin weeps in the rain
> Catherine   if I talked to a fern do you think it would
> answer   if I stopped at your window what
> Hyacinths   I dial a number   soft click
> A thrush glides in slow circles over the brook
> Catherine stands by the fence, watching a leopard
> I call you from fire   in the white wheel
> I give you the valley
>
> Tony McNeill[63]

---

63. Anthony McNeill, *Credences at the altar of cloud*, pp.134-35. McNeill's stops and spaces in this poem and in much of the book from which it comes, have been influenced, he has said in several lecture/readings, by McCoy Tyner, the jazz pianist.

BIBLIOGRAPHY

Since the background/framework material and ideas that make up this study are comparatively new—'there are no Established Authorities!—I have been urged by New Beacon Books, my publishers, to provide a selected Bibliography of the major items used in preparing it. The result is something (along with Notes and Documentation) almost as long, if not longer, than the text. But that's the point. We are not trying to overwhelm anybody and of course you can always skip it. But I hope you'll eventually come back to it after you've read and absorbed the text, okay? Because this *History of the Voice* is only a beginning—and is an invitation and challenge to others to go further and examine and carry forward these ideas which are, in my view, pertinent not only to our developing literature, but to the sociopolitical matrix out of which it comes. I have, you will see, instead of a simplex alphabetical list, provided a classification of my listening/reading resources and hope that the very act of classification in itself will help add shape and shadow to the project. In future, perhaps, an annotated bibliography but that's another story. . . .

The following are the heads of classification . . .

LANGUAGE

Abrahams, Roger D.
  The man of words in the West Indies
  Baltimore : John Hopkins University Press 1983
Alleyne, Mervyn C.
  Comparative Afro-American: an historical-comparative study of English-based Afro-American dialects of the New World
  Ann Arbor : Karoma Publishers Inc., 1980
Alleyne, Mervyn C.
  'The linguistic continuity of Africa in the Caribbean'
  Black Academy Review 1:4 (Winter 1970)
Allsopp, Richard
  Why a Dictionary of Caribbean English usage?
  /Cave Hill : Caribbean Lexicography Project, Circular A 1972/
Bailey, Beryl Loftman
  Creole languages of the Caribbean area
    New York : M. A. Thesis, Columbia University 1953
Bailey, Beryl Loftman
  Jamaican creole syntax: a transformational approach
  Cambridge : Cambridge University Press 1966
Bailey, Beryl Loftman
  A language guide to Jamaica
  New York : Research Institute for the Study of Man 1962
Cassidy, F. G. & LePage, R. B.
  Dictionary of Jamaican English
  Cambridge : Cambridge University Press 1967; new ed 1980
Collymore, Frank A.
  Notes for a glossary of words and phrases of Barbadian dialect
  Bridgetown : The author 1955; with several extensions
D'costa, Jean
  'Language and dialect in Jamaica'
  Jamaica Journal 2 :1 (March 1968)
Holm, John A. and Shilling, Alison W.
  Dictionary of Bahamian English
  Cold Spring, New York : Lexik House 1982
Jekyll, Walter
  Preface to Claude McKay, *Songs of Jamaica*
  Kingston : Aston W. Gardner 1912
LePage, R. B.
  see Cassidy and LePage (1967, 1980)
Lewis, Maureen Warner
  Thesis

Pollard, Velma
'Figurative language in Jamaican creole'
in *Carib* 3 (1983)
Rickford, John R.
A festival of Guianese words
Georgetown : University of Guyana 1978 (Second edition)
St John, Bruce
Introduction to 'Bumbatuk'
in *Revista de letras* 16 (Dec 1972)
Shilling, Alison W.
see Holm and Shilling (1982)
Thomas, J. J.
The theory and practice of creole grammar
Port of Spain : The Chronicle Publishing Co 1869; London and
Port of Spain : New Beacon Books Ltd 1969

LITERATURE

Brown, John (ed)
Leewards: writings past and present
Basseterre, St Kitts : Extra Mural Dept, UCWI 1961
McKay, Claude
Home to Harlem
New York : Harper & Bros 1928
McKay, Claude
A long way from home
New York : Lee Furman, Inc 1937; Arno Press and The New
York Times 1969
McKay, Claude
My green hills of Jamaica
Kingston and Port of Spain : Heinemann Educational Books
(Caribbean) Ltd 1979
Mais, Roger
Brother Man
London : Jonathan Cape 1954; Heinemann Educational Books
Ltd 1974
Naipaul, V. S.
in
Newsweek 18 August 1980
Naipaul, V. S.
Response to Edward Kamau Brathwaite, 'The function of the
writer in the Caribbean'

ACLALS Conference, Mona, January 1971. Transcript
New World Group
'West Indian poetry—a search for voices'
Seminar on *The state of the arts in Jamaica,* UWI, Mona 1965
Scott, Michael
Tom Cringle's log
Edinburgh : Blackwoods Magazine 1834-35. Paris 1836
Walmsley, Anne (ed)
The sun's eye
London : Longmans 1968

LITERARY CRITICISM

Baker, Houston A. Jr (ed)
Reading Black: essays in the criticism of African, Caribbean and Black American literature
Ithaca, New York : Africana Studies & Research Center, Cornell University 1976
Baker, Houston A., Jr
see Fiedler & Baker (1981)
Baugh, Edward (ed)
Critics on Caribbean literature
London : Allen & Unwin 1978
Brathwaite, Edward Kamau
'Sir Galahad and the islands'
Bim 25 (1957), *Iouanaloa* (Castries : Dept of Extra Mural Studies, UWI 1963)
Cooper, Wayne F. (ed)
The passion of Claude McKay
New York : Schocken Books 1973
Fiedler, Leslie & Baker, Houston, A., Jr (eds)
English literature: opening up the canon
Baltimore : The Johns Hopkins University Press 1981
Hamilton, Bruce
review of *New world of the Caribbean* (q.v.)
Bim 25 (1957)
James, Louis
review of Errol Hill, *Man better man* in
CQ 12 : 2 (June 1966)
Johnson, Iris D.
'Louise Bennett and *The Gleaner* (1943-1956)'
Mona : Caribbean Studies Paper, Dept of English, UWI 1982

Kaye, Jacqueline
'The writer in a multicultural society' in
Multicultural Education 9 :1 (London 1980)
Ramchand, Kenneth
'The fate of writing in the West Indies'
Caribbean Review XI : 4 (1982)
Ramchand, Kenneth
The West Indian novel and its background
London : Faber 1970
Wagner, Jean
Les poètes nègres des Etats-Unis (Paris 1962); trans *Black poets of the United States*
Urbana : Univ of Illinois Press 1973
Yates, Frances
The art of memory
London : Routledge 1966

CALIBAN/BROWNING STUDIES

Berdoe, Edward
The Browning cyclopaedia
New York : Barnes & Noble
Brown, E. K.
'The first person : Caliban upon Setebos' in
Modern Language Notes 66 (1951)
Furness, Horace H.
'Criticism on Caliban' in
The Tempest
Gridley, Roy E.
Browning
London : Routledge & Kegan Paul 1972
Honan, Park
Browning's characters
New Haven : Yale Univ Press 1961
Kermode, Frank
Introduction to *The Tempest*
London : The Arden Shakespeare 1954
Lamming, George
The pleasures of exile
London : Michael Joseph 1960
Langbaum, Robert
The poetry of experience: the dramatic monologue in modern

literary tradition
New York : W. W. Norton 1957, 1963
Litzinger, Boyd & Smalley, Donald (eds)
Browning: the critical heritage
New York : Barnes & Noble
Mannoni, O.
Prospero & Caliban . . .
Paris 1950; trans New York : Frederick A. Praeger, Inc 1956
Miller, Betty
Robert Browning: a portrait
London : 1952
Retamar, Roberto
'Caliban : notes towards a discussion of culture in Our America'
in
Massachusetts Review, Winter-Spring 1974
Shaw, George Bernard
on Caliban in Ward (1969) (q.v)
Ward, Maisie
Robert Browning and his world
1969

HISTORY

Craton, Michael
Testing the chains: resistance to slavery in the British West Indies
Ithaca : Cornell University Press 1982
Crump, C. G. & Jacob, E. F. (eds)
The legacy of the Middle Ages
Oxford : The Clarendon Press 1926

EDUCATION

Campbell, Carl
'Education and Black Consciousness : the amazing
Captain J. O. Cutteridge in
Trinidad & Tobago 1921-1942'
Mona : History Seminar Paper, UWI/1981/
Cutteridge, J. O.
Nelson's West Indian Readers (6 books+)
London & Edinburgh : Thomas Nelson & Sons Ltd. 1927-
Royal Reader, The
London

AFRICAN CULTURE

Field, M. J.
Religion & medicine of the Ga people
Accra & London : Oxford University Press 1937

AFRICAN/NEW WORLD CULTURE

Herskovits, M. J.
The myth of the negro past
New York : Harper & Brothers 1958
Lomax, Alan
'Africanisms in New World negro music . . .' in
R. P. Schaedel (ed), *Research & resources of Haiti* (1969),
reprinted in
Vera Rubin & R. P. Schaedel (eds), *The Haitian potential*
New York : Teachers College Press 1975
Mintz, Sidney (ed)
Slavery, colonialism & racism
New York : Norton 1974
Turner, Lorenzo D.
Africanisms in the Gullah dialect
Chicago : Univ of Chicago Press 1949

AFRICAN/CARIBBEAN CULTURE

Africa and the Caribbean
see Crahan & Knight (1979)
Brathwaite, Edward Kamau
'Kumina : the spirit of African survival in Jamaica' in
Jamaica Journal 42 (1978)
Brathwaite, Edward Kamau
*Wars of respect: Nanny, Sam Sharpe and the struggle for
People's Liberation*
Kingston : Agency for Public Information 1977
Crahan, Margaret E. & Knight, Franklin W. (eds)
Africa and the Caribbean: the legacies of a link
Baltimore : The Johns Hopkins University Press 1979
Ford-Smith, Honor
'The performance aspect of kumina ritual'
Mona : Seminar Paper, Dept of English UWI 1976
Fouchard, Jean
Les marrons de la liberté

Paris 1972, trans *The Haitian Maroons*
New York : Edward W. Blyden Press 1981
Genovese, Eugene
Roll, Jordan, roll: the world the slaves made
New York : Pantheon Books/Random House 1972
Knight, Franklin W.
see Crahan & Knight (1979)
Lewis, Maureen Warner
The nkuyu: spirit messengers of the kumina
Mona : Savacou Publications 1977
Montejo, Esteban
Biografia de un cimarron
Havana 1966, trans *The autobiography of a runaway slave*
London : The Bodley Head 1968; New York : Pantheon Books/
Random House 1968
Price, Richard (ed)
Maroon societies . . .
New York : Anchor Books/Doubleday 1973
Queenie, Miss
see Brathwaite (1978), Lewis (1977)
Schuler, Monica
*'Alas alas Kongo': a social history of indentured African
immigration into Jamaica, 1841-1865*
Baltimore : The Johns Hopkins University Press 1980
Tanna, Laura
'African retentions : Yoruba and Kikingo songs in Jamaica'
Jamaica Journal 16 :3 (August 1983)
Wynter, Sylvia
'Jonkonnu in Jamaica . . .'
Jamaica Journal, June 1970

CARIBBEAN CULTURE

Brathwaite, Edward Kamau
Afternoon of the status crow
Mona : Savacou Workingpaper 1 1982; reprinted in Martini
(1983) (q.v)
Brathwaite, Edward Kamau
*Contradictory omens: cultural diversity and integration in the
Caribbean*
Mona : Savacou Publications 1974
Brathwaite, Edward Kamau
The development of creole society in Jamaica 1770-1820

Oxford : The Clarendon Press 1971
Brathwaite, Edward Kamau
Folk culture of the slaves in Jamaica
London & Port of Spain : New Beacon Books Ltd 1970;
new edition 1981
Brathwaite, Edward Kamau
'The love axe/1 : developing a Caribbean aesthetic 1962-1974' in
Baker (1976), loc cit.; *Bim* 61-63 (1977-78)
Brathwaite, Edward Kamau
*Our ancestral heritage: a bibliography of the roots of culture in
the English-speaking Caribbean*
Kingston : Carifesta Committee 1976; Mona : Savacou 1977
Caribbean Quarterly
Trinidad Carnival issue
/St. Augustine/ : CQ 4 : 3 & 4 (1956)
Fanon, Frantz
Les damnés de la terre
Paris 1961, trans *The damned/The wretched of the earth*
Paris : Presence Africaine 1963, New York : Grove Press 1964,
London : MacGibbon & Kee 1964
Fanon, Frantz
Peau noir, masques blancs
Paris 1952, trans *Black skin, White masks*
New York Grove Press 1967; London : MacGibbon & Kee 1968
Harris, Wilson
New World of the Caribbean
Georgetown : Radio Demerara Broadcast Series 1956/57
Hill, Errol
The Trinidad Carnival ...
Austin : Univ of Texas Press 1972
Lamming, George
New World of the Caribbean
Georgetown : Radio Demerara ?1956/57
Lamming, George
The pleasures of exile
London : Michael Joseph 1960
Martini, Jürgen (ed)
Missile & capsule
Bremen : University of Bremen 1983
Maxwell, Marina Omowale
Play mas ...
Port of Spain : The author ?1976
Maxwell, Marina Omowale

'Towards a revolution in the arts'/of the Caribbean/in
Savacou 2 (Sept 1970)
New World of the Caribbean
see Lamming (1956)
Rubin, Vera & Schaedel, Richard P. (eds)
The Haitian potential
New York : Teachers College Press 1975
Walcott, Derek
Introducing reading of 'The star-apple kingdom'
Port of Spain 1978

ORAL TRADITION

Abimbola, Wande (ed)
Yoruba oral tradition: poetry in music, dance and drama
Ile-Ife : Dept of African Languages & Literatures, University of
Ife 1975
Andrzejewski, B. W. & Lewis, I. M. (eds)
Somali poetry: an introduction
Oxford : Clarendon Press 1964
Babalola, S. A.
The content & form of Yoruba ijala
Oxford : Clarendon Press 1966
Beier, Ulli (ed)
Yoruba poetry: an anthology of traditional poems
Cambridge : Cambridge University Press 1970
Bontemps, Arna
see Hughes (1958)
Egudu, R. & Nwoga, D. (eds)
Igbo traditional verse
London : Heinemann Educational Books Ltd 1973
Finnegan, Ruth
Oral literature in Africa
Oxford : Clarendon Press 1970
Finnegan, Ruth
Oral poetry: its nature, significance and social context
Cambridge : Cambridge University Press 1977
Finnegan, Ruth (ed)
Penguin anthology of oral poetry
Harmondsworth : Penguin Books Ltd 1977
Hughes, Langston & Bontemps, Arna (eds)
The book of negro folklore
New York : Dodd, Mead & Co 1958

60

Hurston, Zora Neale
   The sanctified church
   Berkeley : Turtle Island 1981
Jones, LeRoi, now known as Amiri Baraka
   Blues people . . .
   New York : William Morrow & Co 1963;
   London : MacGibbon & Kee 1965
Lewis, I. M.
   see Andrzejewski (1964)
McLuhan, Marshall
   The Gutenberg galaxy
   Toronto : Univ of Toronto Press 1962;
   London : Routledge & Kegan Paul 1962
Murray, Albert
   Stomping the blues
   New York : McGraw-Hill 1976
Nketia, J. H. Kwabena
   Funeral dirges of the Akan people
   Achimota : No pub details 1955
Nketia, J. H. Kwabena
   The music of Africa
   New York : Norton 1974; London : Gollancz 1975
Nwoga
   see Egudu (1973)
Ogot, B. A.
   History of the Southern Luo
   Nairobi : East African Publishing House 1967
Opie, I. & P.
   The lore and language of schoolchildren
   Oxford : Clarendon Press 1967
Rosenberg, Bruce A.
   The art of the American folk preacher
   New York : Oxford University Press 1970
Rothenberg, Jerome (ed)
   *Technicians of the sacred: a range of poetries from Africa,
   America, Asia & Oceania*
   New York : Doubleday & Co Inc 1968
Searle, Chris
   The forsaken lover: white words & black people
   London : Routledge & Kegan Paul 1972
Tedlock, Dennis
   Finding the center: narrative poetry of the Zuni Indians
   New York : Dial Press 1972

Thompson, Paul
  The voice of the past: oral history
  Oxford : Oxford University Press 1978
Vansina, Jan
  De la tradition orale (1961), trans *The oral tradition* ...
  London : Routledge & Kegan Paul 1965
Whiteley, W. H. (ed)
  A selection of African prose: traditional oral texts
  Oxford : Clarendon Press 1964

ORAL TRADITION/CARIBBEAN

Anderson, Izett & Cundall, Frank
  Jamaica Anancy stories
  Kingston : Institute of Jamaica 1910
Beckwith, Martha
  Black roadways: a study of Jamaican folk life
  Chapel Hill : University of North Carolina Press 1929;
  reprint New York : Negro Universities Press 1969
Beckwith, Martha
  Jamaica Anansi stories
  New York : American Folk-lore Society 1924;
  Kraus Reprint Co 1969
Beckwith, Martha
  Jamaica proverbs
  Poughkeepsie, New York : Folklore Foundation 1925;
  reprint New York : Negro Universities Press 1970
Brodber, Erna
  History of the second generation of Jamaican freemen
  Mona : Ph.D. thesis, Dept of History, UWI ?1984
Brodber, Erna
  Life in Jamaica in the early 20th century ...
  Mona : ISER Seminar Paper 1980
Brodber, Erna & Greene, J. Edward
  Roots & Reggae—ideological tendencies in the recent history of Afro-Jamaica
  Mona : ISER Seminar Paper, June 1979
Brown, Patricia
  Brer Anansi/: a study of Mas Utel of St Mary, traditional storyteller/
  Mona : Caribbean Studies Paper, Dept of History, UWI 1974
Clarke, Sebastian
  Jah music: the evolution of popular Jamaican song

62

London : Heinemann Educational Books 1980

Cundall, Frank
see Anderson (1910)

Davis, Stephen & Simon, Peter
Reggae International
New York : R&B 1982

Elder, J. D.
Evolution of the traditional calypso of Trinidad & Tobago ...
/Philadelphia/ : U of Pennsylvania Ph.D. thesis 1966;
Ann Arbor : University Microfilms /1967

Greene, J. Edward
see Brodber (1979)

Harris, Wilson
History, fable & myth in the Caribbean & Guianas
Georgetown : Edgar Mittelholzer Memorial Lecture Series 1970;
also in CQ 16 : 2 (June 1970)

Hewitt, Mary Jane
*A comparative study of Zora Neale Hurston & Louise Bennett
as cultural conservators*
Mona : Ph.D. dissertation in progress, Dept of English &
History, UWI

Jacobs, H. P.
'An early dialect verse' in
Ja Hist Rev 1 : 3 (1948)

Jekyll, Walter
Jamaican song & story...
London : David Nutt 1907; reprint with new introductions
New York : Dover Publications Inc 1966

La Rose, John
'Fallen comet' : a tribute to Michael Smith
London : *The Guardian* 2 Sept 1983

Lewin, Olive
Folk music research in Jamaica
Kingston : Jamaica School of Music (Draft) Paper / ?1967/

Lewin, Olive
Forty folk songs of Jamaica
Washington, D.C. : OAS 1973

Lewin, Olive
Some folk songs of Jamaica
/Kingston : Folk Music Research Unit, Ja School of Music/
1970

Lewin, Olive
'Spotlight on music'

Sunday Gleaner ?1967-
Marshall, Trevor (et al)
  Folk songs of Barbados
  Bridgetown : Macmarson Associates 1981
Reggae International
  see Davis & Simon (1982)
Simon, Peter
  see Davis & Simon (1982)
Smith, Pamela Coleman
  Annancy stories
  New York : Russell 1899
Tanna, Laura
  The art of Jamaican oral narrative performance
  University of Wisconsin-Madison Ph.D. thesis 1980
Warner, Keith Q.
  Kaiso! ... a study of the calypso as oral literature
  Washington, D.C : Three Continents Press 1982
Webster, Shona
  Development of and background to the Jamaica Pantomime
  Mona : Caribbean Studies Paper, UWI 1975
Werner, A.
  Introduction to
  Jekyll, *Jamaican song & story* (1907)

SHANGO TRAIN MUSIC/POSSESSION

Adderley, Julian Cannonball
  'Worksong' on
  Them dirty blues (New York : Riverside Records RLP 12-322, 1960)
Brathwaite, Edward Kamau
  Gods of the Middle Passage
  Mona : Savacou Working Paper 2, 1982;
  version without bibliography in
  Caribbean Review XI : 4 1982
Conjunto Folklorico Nacional de Cuba
  'Rezo y meta de Changó' on
  Conjunto Folklorico Nacional
  (La Habana : Areito LDA-3156, n.d.)
Deren, Maya
  Divine horsemen: the Voodoo gods of Haiti
  London : Thames & Hudson 1953
Forest City Joe

'Train time' (harmonica & vocal) on
Roots of the blues, rec in the field (Arkansas 1959) and ed by
Alan Lomax
(London/Atlantic LTZK 15211)
Franklin, Aretha
'Pullin' '
with the Muscle Shoals Rhythm Section on *Spirit in the dark*
(Atlantic Records SD 8265 /1970/
Gates, Rev J. M.
'Dry bones' (sermon) on
Jazz Vol 1: *The South,* selected from pre-1941 'Race Records' by
Frederick Ramsay, Jr (New York : Folkways Records FJ 2801,
1950)
Kelsey, Rev Samuel
'I'm a witness for my Lord/I'm a royal child' (song/sermon)
with the Congregation of the Temple Church of God and Christ,
Washington, D.C., n.d. on
The Reverend Kelsey (Washington, D.C. : Brunswick Records
OE 9256)
King, Martin Luther
'I have a dream' (sound/sermon) at the Lincoln Memorial,
August 1963 on
In search of freedom (Mercury Records 20119 SMCL)
Lewis, Meade Lux
'Honky tonk train blues' on
Honky tonk train (Riverside Records RLP 8806)
Marley, Bob & The Wailers
'Comin' in from the cold' on
Uprising (Kingston : Tugg Gong Records 1980)
Marley, Bob & The Wailers
'Zion train' on
Uprising, loc cit
Mars, Louis
The crisis of possession in voodoo (trans)
New York : Reed, Cannon & Johnson 1977
Moore, Johnson Lee
'Eighteen hammers' (call & response vocal)
with 12 Mississippi Penitentiary convicts on *Roots of the blues,*
rec in the field (Mississippi 1959) and edited by Alan Lomax on
London/Atlantic Records LTZK 15211
National Dance Theatre Company of Jamaica
'Kumina' on
Traditional songs of the Caribbean (Washington, D.C. :

Organization of American States OAS-005, 1979
Simpson, G. E.
Religious cults of the Caribbean ...
Rio Piedras : Institute of Caribbean Studies, Univ of Puerto Rico
1965; rev & enlarged ed 1970
Terry, Sonny
'Terry's jump' (harmonica, wash-tub bass, washboard) on
Down Home: a portrait of a people. An introduction to negro folk music, USA,
ed Charles Edward Smith rec NYC 1954 by Moses Asch
(Folkways Records FA 26910)

NATION LANGUAGE/CRITICISM

Brathwaite, Edward Kamau
'The African presence in Caribbean literature'
Daedalus Spring 1974; Mintz (1974), loc cit.; *Bim* 65-67
(1979-80)
Brathwaite, Edward Kamau
'Brother Mais'
Tapia 27 Oct 1974; earlier version as Introduction to Roger
Mais, *Brother Man* (London : Heinemann Educational Books
1974)
Brathwaite, Edward Kamau
'Explosion of Caribbean sound poetry'
Caribbean Contact October 1978; *Jamaica Daily News*
6 October 1978
Brathwaite, Edward Kamau
'Jazz and the West Indian novel'
Bim 44-46 (1967-68)
Figueroa, John
'Our complex language situation' in
Caribbean voices, ed Figueroa (London : Evans 1970)
Foligno, Cesare
'Vernacular literature' in
The legacy of the Middle Ages, (see Crump & Jacob 1926)
Glissant, Edouard
'Free and forced poetics' in
Alcheringa 2 (1976)
Henderson, Stephen
Understanding the new Black poetry: Black speech & Black music as poetic references
New York : William Morrow & Co, Inc 1973

Jacobs, H. P.
'The dialect of Victor Reid'
West Indian Review (May 1949)
Laird, Christopher
An Introduction to Bruce St John at Kairi House/in
bruce st john at kairi house (1974, 1975)
Morris, Mervyn
Introduction
Louise Bennett, *Selected poems* (1982)
Morris, Mervyn
Sleeve note
Miss Lou! live (1983)
Morris, Mervyn
'On reading Louise Bennett, seriously'
Sunday Gleaner, June 7-28 1965; *Jamaica Journal* 1 : 1
(December 1967)
Morris, Mervyn
'People speech /5 dub poets of Jamaica/'
Reggae International (1982)
Nettlefold, Rex
Introduction
Louise Bennett, *Jamaica labrish* (1966)
Ramchand, Kenneth
'Dialect in West Indian fiction' in
CQ 14 (1968) and in *The West Indian novel and its background*
(London : Faber 1970)
Rohlehr, Gordon
'Calypso & morality'
Moko 17 June 1969
Rohlehr, Gordon
'Calypso & politics'
Moko 29 Oct 1971
Rohlehr, Gordon
'The calypso as rebellion'
S.A.G 3 (1970)
Rohlehr, Gordon
'The folk in Caribbean literature'
Tapia 17 December 1972
Rohlehr, Gordon
'Forty years of calypso'
Tapia 3 & 17 Sept, 8 Oct 1972
Rohlehr, Gordon
Pathfinder: Black awakening in The arrivants of Edward Kamau

Brathwaite
Tunapuna, Trinidad : The author 1981
Rohlehr, Gordon
'Samuel Selvon & the language of the people' in
Baugh, loc cit
Rohlehr, Gordon
'Sounds & pressure : Jamaican blues' in
Cipriani Labour College Review, June 1970
Rohlehr, Gordon
'Sparrow and the language of calypso' in
Savacou 2 (1970). See also *CAM Newsletters* 3, 4 (1967), 6 (1968)
Rohlehr, Gordon
'West Indian poetry—some problems of assessment' in
Tapia 29 August 1971, CQ 17 : 2&3 (1971), *Bim* 54, 55 (1972)

NATION LANGUAGE/MUSIC

Big Youth
Everyday skank
London : Trojan Records TRLS 189, 1980 (rec 1972)
Big Youth
Screamin target
Kingston : Dynamic Sounds Jaguar Jag 5408, 1972
Drummond, Don
In memory of Don Drummond
Kingston : Studio One ?1965
Marley, Bob & The Wailers
'Duppy Conqueror' on
Kingston : Upsetter EP ?1968; *African Herbsman* (1969),
Burnin' (1973)
Shadow
'Bass Man'
New York : Straker's Records GS 132 A, ?1972
Short Shirt
'Tourist leggo'
Kingston : Dynamic Sounds Ltd/Weed Beat WB 031, 1976
Sparrow, The Mighty
'Dan is the man in the van'
Port of Spain : National Recording Co Ltd.
EP ?1958
Sparrow, The Mighty
'How you jammin' so' on
Sparrow vs The Rest (Kingston : Dynamic Sounds/Tysett

SHW 1976-1, 1976
Sparrow, The Mighty
  'Music & Rhythm' on
  Sparrow vs The Rest, q.v.
Sparrow, The Mighty
  'Ten to one is murder'
  Port of Spain : National Recording Co Ltd., EP 1960
Sweet Honey in the Rocks
  Good News
  Chicago : Flying Fish 245, 1981

NATION LANGUAGE/PERFORMANCES

Bennett, Louise
Cliff, Jimmy
  The harder they come (film)
  Kingston 1972
Dem Two/All A We
Gomez, Pandora
Jamaica Pantomime
Keane, Shake
Keens-Douglas, Paul
Malik
  The bad poet
  Port of Spain 1975
Malik
  Overview 1980
  St Georges, Grenada 1980
Malik
  Revolution
  Port of Spain 1975
Malik
  Visionera—view from the pitch
Malik
  The whirlwind
  Port of Spain 1977
St John, Bruce
Sistren
  Bandaalu version
  Kingston : Barn Theatre 1979
Sistren
  Bellywoman Bangarang
  Kingston : Barn Theatre 1978

Sistren
  QPH
  Kingston : Barn Theatre 1981
Smith, Michael
  'Upon Westminster Bridge'
  BBC 2 TV (1982) Arena programme

NATION LANGUAGE/RECORDINGS

Atwell, Melvin
  see St John
Anthology of negro poets
  see Bontemps (1966)
Baraka, Imamu Amiri/Jones, LeRoi
  'Beautiful black women' on
  Black & Beautiful/Soul Madness (?Newark, N.J. : Jihad
  Productions 1001, ?1966
Baraka
  'Black Art' on
  Sonny Murray, *Sonny 'Stime Now* (?Newark, N.J. : Jihad
  Productions 663, ?1965
Baraka
  'Black Dada Nihilissimus' with
  The New York Art Quarter (New York : ESP-1004, 1965)
Baraka
  It's nation time
  Detroit : Black Forum/Motown B 455L, 1972
Baraka
  New music—New Poetry (with David Murray, ten & bass clt,
  Steve McCall, drs)
  New York : India Navigation IN-1048, 1981
Bennett, Louise
  Miss Lou! live . . .
  London : Island Records; Kingston : IManI Records 1983
Bennett, Louise
  Miss Lou's views
  Kingston : Federal Records Federal 204, ?1966
Bernard, Eulalia
  Negritud/Poesia Negra Costarricense
  ?San José Imprenta Imperial PP-420, c1976

Bongo Jerry
  'Mabrak'
  Kingston : Yard Theatre/Groundation 1969 (EKB tape)
Bongo Jerry
  Tribute to Don Drummond
  see Hussey (1969, 1980)
Bontemps, Arna (ed)
  Anthology of negro poets
  New York : Folkways Records FL 9791, 1966
Brodber, Erna
  History of the second generation of Jamaican freemen
  Mona : ISER Tape Archive 1980
Brathwaite, Edward Kamau
  'Caliban' on
  Islands (London : Argo Records PLP 1184/5, 1973
Brathwaite, Edward Kamau
  'Calypso' on
  Rights of passage (London : Argo Records DA 101 (1969),
  PLP 1110 (?1972)
Brathwaite, Edward Kamau
  'The Dust' on
  Rights of passage (London : Argo Records DA 102 (1969),
  PLP 1111 (?1972)
Brathwaite, Edward Kamau
  'Nametracks' on
  Mother Poem (ATCAL/University of Warwick reading. Tape
  1980
Brathwaite, Edward Kamau
  'Rites' (Cricket) on
  Islands, loc cit
Brathwaite, Edward Kamau
  'So come/quick cattle/train' on
  Rights of passage, loc cit
Brown, Sterling
  'Ma Rainey, on
  Anthology of negro poets
Fabio, Sarah W.
  Boss soul: 12 poems . . . set to drum talk, rhythms & images
  New York : Folkways Records FL 9710, 1972
Figueroa, John
  'Portrait of a woman' on
  Poets of the West Indies reading their own works
  (New York : Caedmon Records TC 1379, 1971)

Guillen, Nicholas
  Nicolas Guillen dice sus poemas
  /Havana/ : EGRM LD-101, n.d
Guillen, Nicolas
  'Sensemaya'
Hinkson, Anthony
  'Janet'
  EKB tape, Erdiston Teachers College, Bridgetown 1973
Hughes, Langston
  The Black verse/12 moods for jazz /a reading of Ask Your Mama/
  ?New York : Buddah Records BDS 2005, n.d
Hughes, Langston
  Weary blues
  New York : MGM Records Verve VSP/VSPS-36, 1958
Hussey, Dermott (prod)
  Requiem for Don Drummond
  Kingston : RJR Radio 1969; rev version JBC Radio 1980
Johnson, Linton Kwesi
  Bass culture
  London : Island Records ILPS 9605, 1980
Johnson, Linton Kwesi
  Dread beat an blood
  London : Virgin Records FL 1017, 1978
Jones, LeRoi, *see* Baraka
Keane, Shake
  'Nancitori'
  Georgetown : Carifesta 72 tape (EKB), 1972
Keens-Douglas, Paul
  'I ball' on
  One to One/Paul Keens-Douglas live at the Little Carib
  (Port of Spain : Keensdee Records PK-D 003, 1978
Keens-Douglas, Paul
  'Pan Rap I, II' on
  Is Town say so! (Port of Spain : Keensdee Records PK-D 005, 1982
Keens-Douglas, Paul
  'Sugar George' on
  "Tim Tim" (Port of Spain : Keensdee Records PK-D 001, ?1975
Keens-Douglas, Paul
  'Tanti at de Oval' on
  "Tim Tim"
Keens-Douglas, Paul

'Wukhand' on
"Tim Tim"
Lamming, George
Reading 'On this night' by Geo Campbell on
New World of the Caribbean, loc cit
Malcolm X
Message to the grass roots
Detroit : Afro-American Broadcasting & Recording Co Afro
Records AA-1264, 1965 : (Malcolm's last speech)
Malik
More Power to the nation: the poetry & music of Malik
Port of Spain : The poet 1981/82
Matthews, Marc
Marc-up/Marc Matthews and friends—live
/Bridgetown/ : A TIE Production, WIRL Records T.I.E W087,
1987
Mutabaruka
Check it
Kingston : Tuff gong 1983; Chicago : Alligator Records AL 8306
Oku Onuora/Wong, Orlando
I a tell/Reflection in red/Reflection in dub
Kingston : Kuya SK 001 (12in 45rpm), ?1982
Oku Onuora/Wong, Orlando
Parole Prison reading at HQ of Jamaica Lib Service, Tom
Redcam Avenue, Kingston, September 1977 (EKB tape rec)
Pietri, Pedro
Loose joints
New York : Folkways Records FL 9722 (1979)
Pool, Rosey (ed)
Beyond the blues: American negro poetry . . .
London : Argo Record Co Ltd RG 338, 1963
Pragnell, Alfred
Reading 'Telephone conversation' by Jeannette Layne Clarke on
Laughin' sport (Bridgetown : Merry Disc EP) 1973
Roses & Revolutions
A celebration of Afro-American word/song, with Osceola Adams,
Ruby Dee, Roberta Flack, Ellan Holly, Lena Horne, Novella
Nelson, Leontyne Price, Barbara Ann Teer, Leslie Uggams,
Nancy Wilson, Aretha Franklin, Roscoe Lee Browne (Washing-
ton, D.C. : D.S.T. Telecommunications Inc., ?1975
St John, Bruce
'Bajan Litany' on (with Atwell)
The foetus pains (Bridgetown : WIRL (Barbados), Trex Records

(EP45) B 205, /1972/
St John, Bruce
'Cricket' on
The foetus pleasures (Bridgetown : **WIRL** (Barbados), **WIRL**
B 227, 1973
St John, Bruce
'Education' (with Atwell)
The foetus pains
St John, Bruce
'Subtlety'
The foetus pleasures
Sanchez, Sonia
A sun lady for all seasons
New York : Folkways FL 9793, 1971
Scott, Dennis
'Uncle Time' on
Poets of the West Indies
Smith, Michael
'Lang time' on
Mi cyaan believe it (London : Island Records 1982;
New York : Mango 1982
Smith, Michael
'Mi cyaan believe it' on
Word Sound (Kingston : Light of Saba 002, 1978, reissued
London : LKJ Records LJK 001 (Disco 45) ?1981
Smith, Michael
'Mi cyaan believe it' on
Mi cyaan believe it
Smith, Michael
'Trainer' on
Mi cyaan believe it
Thompson, Tony
Fuzzi's sermon
EKB tape Bridgetown 1973, Mona (carifesta) 1979
Utel, Mas
Ananse stories
Pat Brown tape, St Mary 1974
Walcott, Derek
'Blues' on
Poetry International '69, q.v
Walcott, Derek
'The glory trumpeter' on
Poets of the West Indies, loc cit

Walcott, Derek
  'The schooner *Flight*' on
  The schooner, Flight & other poems
  (Port of Spain : The Parla Publishing Co Ltd ?1980

NATION LANGUAGE POETRY TEXTS

Anon
  'Helena'
  Jamaica folk song in *Jamaica Jour* 8 : 2&3 (1974)
Bennett, Louise
  Jamaica labrish
  Kingston : Sangster's Book Stores 1966
Bennett, Louise
  Selected poems, ed Mervyn Morris
  Kingston : Sangster's Book Stores 1982
Bloom, Valerie
  Touch mi, tell mi!
  London : Bogle-L'Ouverture 1983
Bongo Jerry
  'Mabrak' in
  Savacou 3/4 (1970/71)
Bongo Jerry
  'Roll on, Sweet Don' in
  Abeng 17 May 1969
Brathwaite, Edward Kamau
  The arrivants
  London : Oxford University Press 1973
Brathwaite, Edward Kamau
  Black + Blues
  Havana : Casa de las Americas 1976
Brathwaite, Edward Kamau
  Islands
  London : Oxford University Press 1969
Brathwaite, Edward Kamau
  Mother poem
  Oxford : Oxford University Press 1977
Brathwaite, Edward Kamau
  Rights of passage
  London : Oxford University Press 1967
Brathwaite, Edward Kamau (ed)
  Savacou 3/4: New writing (1970/71)

Brathwaite, Edward Kamau (ed)
  Savacou 14/15: New poets from Jamaica (1979/80)
Brathwaite, Edward Kamau
  Sun poem
  Oxford : Oxford University Press 1982
Brathwaite, Edward Kamau
  Third world poems
  London : Longman Drumbeat 1983
Brown, Sterling
  Collected Poems . . .
  New York : Harper & Row 1980
Brown, Sterling
  Southern Road
  New York : Harcourt, Brace 1932
Clarke, Jeannette Layne (as Layne)
  'Telephone conversation' in
  Bim 47 (1968)
Collymore, Frank
  'Voice la plume de mon oncle' in
  Collected poems (Bridgetown : Advocate Co 1959)
Cordle, Edward A.
  *Overheard: a series of poems written by the late Edward A.
  Cordle and published in the columns of The Weekly Recorder*
  Bridgetown : C. F. Cole 1903
Figueroa, John
  'Portrait of a woman' in
  Savacou 3/4 (1970/71), *Ignoring hurts* (Washington, D.C :
  Three Continents Press 1976)
Figueroa, John
  'Problems of a writer who does not quite . . .' in
  Ambit 91 (1982)
Guillen, Nicolas
  Antologia major
  La Habana : Union 1964; 2nd edition La Habana : Instituto del
  libro 1969
Guillen, Nicolas
  West Indies, Ltd
  La Habana : Ucar Garcia 1934
Guillen, Nicolas
  The Great Zoo and other poems
  trans & edited Robert Marquez
  New York : Monthly Review Press 1972
Guillen, Nicolas

Man-making words: selected poems . . .
Trans & ed Robert Marquez and David Arthur McMurray
Amherst : University of Massachusetts Press 1972
Guillen, Nicolas
Motivos de son
La Habana : Rambla, Bouza y Cia 1930
Guillen, Nicolas
Songoro cosongo: poemas mulatos
La Habana : Ucar Garcia y Cia 1931
Guillen, Nicolas
West Indies, Ltd
La Habana : Ucar Garcia 1934
Hill, Errol (ed)
Caribbean plays, vol 2
/St Augustine/ : Dept of Extra Mural Studies, UWI 1965
Hill, Errol
'Dance Bongo' in
Caribbean plays, loc cit
Hill, Errol
Man better man in
John Gassner (ed), *Yale School of Drama presents . . .*
(New York : E. P. Dutton & Co., Inc 1968)
Hill, Errol (ed)
A time . . . and a season: 8 Caribbean plays
/St Augustine/ : Extramural Studies Unit, UWI 1976
Hill, Errol (ed)
West Indian plays
/St Augustine/ : Extra-Mural Dept, UCWI 1958
Hinkson, Anthony
Slavation
Bridgetown : unpub coll c1976
Johnson, James Weldon
God's trombones: seven negro sermons in verse
New York : The Viking Press 1927
Johnson, Linton Kwesi
Dread beat and blood
London : Bogle-L'Ouverture 1975
Johnson, Linton Kwesi
Inglan is a bitch
London : Race Today Publications 1980
Jones, Evan
'Lament of the banana man' in
Independence anthology of Jamaican literature (1962), loc cit

77

Jones, Evan
  'Song of the banana man' in
  Independence anthology of Jamaican literature
Keane, Shake
  Nancitori/with drums
  Kingston, St Vincent : The author 1972
Keane, Shake
  One a week with water
  La Habana : Casa de las Americas 1979
Keane, Shake
  'Shaker funeral' in
  L'oubli (/Bridgetown : The author ?1950)
Keens-Douglas, Paul
  Is Town say so!
  Port of Spain : Keensdee Productions 1981
Keens-Douglas, Paul
  Tell me again
  Port of Spain : Keensdee Productions 1979
Keens-Douglas, Paul
  "Tim Tim"
  [Port of Spain] : The author 1976
Keens-Douglas, Paul
  When moon shine
  /Port of Spain/ : The author 1975
Laird, Christopher
  'Hosay' in
  Kairi 2.74
McKay, Claude
  Constab ballads
  London : Watts 1912
McKay, Claude
  Songs from Jamaica
  London : Augener 1912
McKay, Claude
  Songs of Jamaica
  Kingston : Aston W. Gardner 1912
McNeill, Anthony
  Letters poems/ in
  Credences at the altar of cloud (Kingston : Institute of Jamaica
  1979)
McNeill, Anthony
  'Ode to Brother Joe' in
  Reel from "The life-movie" (Mona : Savacou Publications 1975)

Malik
Black up
Curepe, Trinidad : Priv pub 1972
Malik
Revo
Tunapuna, Trinidad : Priv pub /1975/
Millington, N. Roy
'On return from a foreign land' in
Lingering thoughts (/Bridgetown/ : Priv pub 1954)
Morris, Mervyn
'Valley Prince'/for Don Drummond/ in
Savacou 3/4 (1970/71), *The pond* (London & Port of Spain :
New Beacon Books 1973)
Nunn, Ann
'/Poem/ for Anguilla after Hurricane 'Donna',
September 1960' in
Leewards, loc cit
Pool, Rosey E. (ed)
Beyond the blues
Lympne, Kent : The Hand & Flower Press 1962
Queenie, Miss
Kumina
see Brathwaite (1978), Warner Lewis (1977)
Questel, Victor D.
'Man dead' in
Near mourning ground, loc cit
Questel, Victor D.
'Near mourning ground' in
Near mourning ground, loc cit
Questel, Victor D.
'Shaka's cycle' in
Near mourning ground, loc cit
St John, Bruce
bruce st john at kairi house
Port of Spain : Kairi 4/5, 1974; 2nd edition kairi 1975
Scott, Dennis
'Uncle Time' in
Focus 1960; *Uncle Time* (/Pittsburgh/ : Univ of Pittsburgh Press
1973)
Scott, Michael
Tom Cringle's log/verses in
Edinburgh : *Blackwood's Magazine* Sept 1829-August 1833;
Paris 1836

Sherlock, Philip
  'Pocomania' in
  Focus 1943
Sherlock, Philip
  Shout for freedom: a tribute to Sam Sharpe
  London & Basingstoke : Macmillan Caribbean 1976
Smith, Michael
  Mi cyaan believe it/poems on back of sleeve
  London : Island Records 1983
Sparrow, The Mighty
  One hundred and twenty calypsoes to remember . . .
  Port of Spain : National Recording Co 1963
Walcott, Derek
  'Blues' in
  The Gulf (London 1969, New York 1970)
Walcott, Derek
  'The glory trumpeter' in
  Selected poems (New York 1964); *The castaway* (London 1965)
Walcott, Derek
  'Parang' in
  In a green night (London 1962); *Selected poems*
  (New York 1964)
Walcott, Derek
  'Pocomania' in
  In a green night (1962); *Selected poems* (1964)
Walcott, Derek
  'Poopa, da' was a fete' in
  In a green night (1962); *Selected poems* (1964)
Walcott, Derek
  'The schooner *Flight*' in
  The star-apple kingdom (New York 1979, London 1980)
Walcott, Derek
  'The Spoiler's return' in
  The fortunate traveller (New York 1981, London 1982)

POETRY TEXTS (NOT NATION) CONNECTED
WITH THE STUDY

Alexander, Michael (trans & ed)
  The earliest English poems
  Harmondsworth : Penguin Books Ltd 1966
Anon
  Beowulf
  c 700

Anon
The seafarer
Blake, William
Songs of experience
London 1794
Blake, William
Songs of innocence
London 1789
Brown, John (ed)
Leewards: writings, past & present ...
/Basseterre, St Kitts/ : Dept of Extra-Mural Studies,
UCWI 1961
Browning, Robert
'Caliban upon Setebos' in
Dramatis personae (London 1864)
Campbell, George
'On this night' in
First poems (/Kingston/ : Priv pub 1945; new rev & enlarged ed
New York : Garland Publishing Inc 1981)
Cesaire, Aimé
Cahier d'un retour au pays natal
Paris 1939; Presence Africaine 1965; trans *Return to my native
land*
(New York : Brentano's 1947; Paris : Presence Africaine 1968;
London : Penguin Books 1969)
Cesaire, Aimé
The collected poetry
trans, intro, notes Clayton Eshleman & Annette Smith
Berkeley : Univ of California Press 1983
Chapman, M. J.
Barbadoes and other poems
London : James Fraser 1833
Chaucer
The canterbury tales
?London 1387-
Clarke, Leroy
Douens: poems & drawings
/New York/ : KaRaEle 1981
Collymore, Frank
Collected poems
Bridgetown : Priv pub 1959
cummings, e. e.
selected poems 1923-1958

London : Faber 1960

Depestre, René
Un arc-en-ciel pour l'occident chretien
Paris 1967; trans *A rainbow for the Christian West*
Amherst : U of Mass Press 1977

Eliot, T. S.
Collected poems 1909-1935
London : Faber 1936

Ensor, R. C. K.
Columbus, a historical poem . . .
London : Secker 1925

Figueroa, John (ed)
Caribbean voices /:an anthology/
London : Evans 1970; combined ed from *Dreams & visions*
(1966), *The blue horizons* (1970)

Figueroa, John
Ignoring hurts . . .
Washington, D.C : Three Continents Press 1976

Gray, Thomas
Elegy written in a country courtyard
London : Dodsley 1751

Harris, Wilson
Eternity to season
/Georgetown/ : The author 1954; new edition London & Port
of Spain : New Beacon Books 1978

Hendriks, A. L. & Lindo, Cedric (eds)
The Independence anthology of Jamaican literature
/Kingston/ : The Arts Celebration Cttee of the Min of Dev &
Welfare 1962

Hopkins, Gerard Manley
Poems . . .
London : Oxford Univ Press 1930

Keane, Shake
L'oubli
Bridgetown : The author 1950

Langland, William
The vision concerning Piers the Plowman
?London c 1362

Leewards
See Brown (1961)

Lindo, Cedric (ed)
see Hendriks & Lindo (1962)

McFarlane, J. E. Clare (ed)

A treasury of Jamaican poetry
London : University of London Press 1949

McKay, Claude
Selected poems
New York : Bookman Associates 1953; reprint New York :
Harcourt, Brace & World 1969

McNeill, Anthony
Credences at the altar of cloud
Kingston : Institute of Jamaica 1979

McNeill, Anthony
Reel from "The life-movie"
Mona : Savacou Publications Ltd 1972; revised 1975

Millington, N. Roy
Lingering thoughts
Bridgetown : Priv pub 1954

Milton
Paradise lost
London 1667; rev 1674

Moore, Marianne
Collected poems
London : Faber 1951

Neruda, Pablo
The heights of Macchu Picchu
London : Cape 1966; trans Nathaniel Tarn

Palgrave, F. T.
The golden treasury 'selected from the best songs & lyrical poems
in the English language'
London 1861; with continuing editions . . .

Plath, Sylvia
Ariel
London : Faber 1965

Questel, Victor D.
Near mourning ground
Diego Martin, Trinidad : The New Voices 1979

Seymour, A. J.
'For Christopher Columbus' in
The Guiana Book

Seymour, A. J.
The Guiana Book
Georgetown : The author 1948

Seymour, A. J.
Over Guiana, clouds
Georgetown : The author 1944

Shakespeare, William
 The Tempest
 ?1610
Shelley, Percy Bysshe
 'Ode to the West Wind'
 1820
Smith, M. G.
 'Jamaica' in
 The Independence anthology of Jamaican literature
Telemaque, H. M.
 'In our land' in
 H. M. Telemaque & A. M. Clarke, *Burnt bush*
 (Port of Spain : Fraser's Printerie 1947)
Tennyson, Alfred, Lord
 The Princess
 London 1847
Vaughan, H. A.
 'Revelation' in
 Sandy Lane and other poems
Vaughan, H. A.
 Sandy Lane and other poems
 Bridgetown : Priv pub 1945
Walcott, Derek
 Another life
 New York : Farrar, Straus & Giroux 1973, London : Cape 1973,
 Washington, D.C : Three Continents 1982
Walcott, Derek
 The castaway
 London : Cape 1965
Walcott, Derek
 Epitaph for the young
 Bridgetown : The author 1949
Walcott, Derek
 The fortunate traveller
 New York : Farrar, Straus & Giroux 1981, London : Faber 1982
Walcott, Derek
 The gulf
 London : Cape 1969, New York : Farrar, Straus & Giroux 1970
Walcott, Derek
 In a green night
 London : Cape 1962
Walcott, Derek
 'Sambo Agonistes' in

Bim 15 (1951)
Walcott, Derek
  Selected poems
  New York : Farrar & Straus 1964
Walcott, Derek
  The star-apple kingdom
  New York : Farrar, Strauss & Giroux 1979
Walcott, Derek
  25 poems
  Bridgetown : The author 1949
Whitman, Walt
  Leaves of grass
  1855
Wordsworth, William
  Lyrical ballads
  London 1798

POETS VOICES
(recordings other than those inc under nation)

Caedmon treasury of modern poets reading their own poetry
  New York : Caedmon TC 0994, 0995
  inc Yeats, Auden, Sitwell, Dylan Thomas, MacNiece, Graves,
  Gertrude Stein, MacLeish, Cummings, Marianne Moore,
  Empson, Spender, Aiken
Collymore, Frank
  'Voice la plume de mon oncle'
  Poets of the West Indies
Eliot, T. S.
  Four quartets
  London : HMV CLP 1115, n.d
Eliot, T. S.
  T. S. Eliot reading Poems & Choruses
  New York : Caedmon TC 1045; rec London 1955
Eliot, T. S.
  The waste land / and other poems
  New York : Caedmon TC 1326, n.d
Figueroa, John (ed)
  Poets of the West Indies reading their own works
  New York : Caedmon TC 1379, rec c1970
  inc McNeill, Scott, Morris, Walcott, Brathwaite, Collymore,
  Roach, Figueroa, Vaughan

First International Book Fair of Radical Black & Third World
    Books
    An evening of international poetry
    London : Alliance Records PLP 001, March 1982
    inc Agard (Guyana), Berry (Ja), Bloom (Ja), Brathwaite (B'dos),
    Accabre Huntley (Black Britain), Linton Kwesi Johnson (Ja),
    Laird (T'dad), Markham (Montserrat), Mapanje (Malawi),
    Onuora (Ja), Okot p'Bitek (Uganda), Rajendra (Malaysia),
    Sarduy (Cuba), Mushtaq Singh (Pakistan), Michael Smith (Ja),
    Fred Williams (Ja)
Gielgud, John
    reading 'Ode to the West Wind' on *The voice of poetry*
    London : Columbia 78 DB 1887, n.d
Ginsberg, Allen
    readings
Hughes, Ted
    Selections from Crow & Wodwo
    New York : Caedmon TC 1628, n.d
Henri, Adrian & McGough, Roger
    the Incredible new Liverpool scene
    London : CBS BPG 53045, 1957
Lamming, George
    reading George Campbell's 'On this night' on
    New World of the Caribbean, loc cit
McGough, Roger
    see Henri & McGough (1957)
McKay, Claude
    reading on *Anthology of negro poets,* loc cit
McNeill, Anthony
    reading from *Credences at the altar of cloud*
    Mona : UWI (Radio Unit tape)
Orr, Peter (ed)
    The poet speaks 5
    London : Argo RG 455
    inc Ted Hughes (1962), Porter (1963), Gunn (1965), Plath (1962)
Orr, Peter (ed)
    The poet speaks 10
    London : Argo Records RG 583
    inc Blunden, Muir, Grigson, Wain, Abse, Barker, Graham,
    Logue, Lucie-Smith, Brathwaite
Orr, Peter (ed)
    Poetry international '69
    London : Argo Records MPR 262, 263, 1969

inc Auden, Holub, Austin, Clarke, Pilinszky, Yannis Ritsos,
Ogden Nash, Bly, Brathwaite, Walcott, Vasko Popa
Poets of the West Indies
  see Figueroa (ed)
Thomas, Dylan
  readings
Vaughan, H. A.
  reading on *Poets of the West Indies*
Voznesensky
  readings

BBC
  Caribbean Evening
  London : BBC 3 (January 1979)
  a series of 12 half-hour programmes of Caribbean cultural ex-
  pression, recorded in the Caribbean and London, produced by
  Joan Griffiths
  Caribbean Voices
  London : Caribbean Service (1943-1958)
  the single most important literary catalyst for Caribbean creative
  and critical writing in English : 15 half-hour weekly years : a
  most significant contribution to and confirmation of our oral
  tradition though, alas, the BBC has (had to) scrub(bed) this
  tremendous archive. The scripts, however, have been deposited
  with the UWI Library, Mona. Una Marson, George Lamming,
  Sam Selvon, Edgar Mittelholzer, Andrew Salkey, Vidia Naipaul,
  Shake Keane and Edward Kamau Brathwaite, among many,
  many others, were associated with the programme; the very first
  reader was Cameron Tudor. The most influential producer
  (drive, enthusiasm, sympathy, critical acumen and length of
  service) was Henry Swanzy